READY-TO-GO
REPRODUCIBLES

Punctuation

Puzzles & Mazes

By Jim Halverson

Grades 4–8

SCHOLASTIC
PROFESSIONAL **B**OOKS

New York • Toronto • London • Auckland • Sydney
Mexico City • New Delhi • Hong Kong

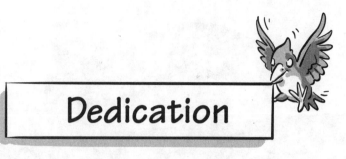

Dedication

My colleagues at Saint Ann's School asked for and inspired this book and its two companions, my students (no-nonsense editors!) enthusiastically helped me revise all three, and my family, dear Anita and Leif, supported and encouraged and often suffered through the writing process over several long years.

Cover design by Kelli Thompson
Interior design by Grafica, Inc.
Interior illustrations by Dave Clegg

ISBN 0-439-05188-6

Table of Contents

Introduction

What This Book Is...

The exercises in this book rest upon two assumptions: that students learn best when they are having fun, and that most students need frequent repetition of punctuation concepts in order to retain them. These units are designed to help you address both needs. Instead of taking another punctuation quiz to test and demonstrate their knowledge, students get to solve word puzzles, mazes, and picture mysteries.

The exercises are also designed to suit a range of teaching needs. They can be used by an entire class or for individual enrichment, and they reflect varying age and skill levels. Many units have three separate exercises, each a bit harder and more sophisticated than the one before it. You may find that only one of these is appropriate for the age level of the students you teach, or you may wish to work your way up through all of them.

...And Is Not

The introduction to each unit provides helpful definitions, rules, examples, and a mini-lesson. However, these introductions are not designed to be complete teaching guides. Similarly, the exercises are meant to supplement your teaching, not to provide a complete or methodical program for each concept. For easier punctuation rules, you may find that the exercises here are sufficient, but for stubborn problems, such as sentence fragments and run-ons, you are surely going to want to build up to these exercises with preliminary work. You can then use these mazes and games as enjoyable rewards for mastering the concepts.

Before You Start...

Since the exercises require that students have a working knowledge of the concepts involved, it is very important for you to familiarize yourself with a unit before using it. Make sure that you have cov-
ered all the punctuation decisions that crop up. Within the unit, check the degree of difficulty of the exercises and decide which pages best suit your students. Generally, the first page is probably best for fourth or fifth grades, the second for fifth or sixth grades, and the third for seventh or eighth grades, but these can be only very rough guidelines since classes vary so greatly. A few units that deal with difficult concepts like adjective and adverb clauses have only two exercises for older students; similarly, the review units at the end are intended for more sophisticated classes.

...And After You Finish

I hope that you will connect the grammar activity pages in this book with real-world writing and help students see that an understanding of punctuation and capitalizaton is really just a small part of a bigger picture—written communication. The sooner they can make a punctuation concept "theirs" by seeing it at work in their own writing, the sooner that punctuation concept will be theirs for life. For instance, after students work on exercises from the units on adjective and adverb clauses, you might give a writing assignment that asks them to vary their style by including at least five sentences with adverb clauses and five with adjective clauses, all correctly punctuated. Or after doing a proper-noun exercise you might have younger students proofread their own writing for capitalization errors by pretending that they are detectives looking for mistakes that a suspect may have made.

Finally, don't forget that using good punctuation is just one of many writing skills and not an end in itself. Some of your students—some of us!—are going to continue to make capitalization and punctuation mistakes, but those lapses should not prevent them from being appreciated as fine writers when their written communication is fresh, vivid, forceful, or delightful.

—Jim Halverson

Unit 1: Capitalization Rules

Units 1 and 2 are designed to help students apply capitalization rules effectively. Unit 2 asks students to consider context, while this one deals exclusively with words that are almost always proper nouns and proper adjectives.

Definition: A *proper noun* names a specific person, place, or thing and is written with an initial capital letter; a *proper adjective* is a modifier formed from a proper noun. A *common noun* or *common adjective* represents or describes a non-specific person, place, or thing and begins with a lowercase letter.

Example: Doctor Francis, who speaks French, fixed my fractured femur on Friday.

Teaching Tips

★ Capitalization rules in English continue to change! Even as this book is being written, some words are probably moving from proper to common status. Only recently the highest elected official in the United States was demoted to *president* from *President*. If you read a lot of nineteenth-century literature, you may still find yourself wanting to capitalize the names of the seasons. (For some reason students still write *Spring* and *Fall* but rarely *Summer* or *Winter*.)

Here is a list of categories of proper nouns and adjectives that, it seems safe to say, will still need to be capitalized many decades from now:

Proper Nouns & Adjectives	Examples
languages	French
religions	Islam
days of the week	Tuesday
months	January
holidays	Thanksgiving
brand names	Ford
countries	Ghana
nationalities	Irish
geographical names	Grand Canyon
organizations and institutions	Elks Club, Coe College
ships	*The Queen Mary*
planets	Jupiter

Capitalization Rules

★ If you teach students who are bilingual, especially if they also write a European language, you should emphasize that there are significant capitalization differences between English and other languages.

Problematic Common Nouns & Adjectives	Correct Examples
seasons	spring
animals and birds	lion, eagle
professions	doctor
school subjects (except languages)	history (English)
directions (unless a region's name)	south (the South)

Of course, many words that fit into the list above become proper nouns when they are used as names or titles, such as *Doctor* Jones (a person's title and name) and *History* II (a course title).

Mini-Lesson

You can make learning proper nouns and adjectives into a game to heighten student involvement. Hold up a folded sheet of paper and tell the class that you have written a number on it. You want to see how many of them can determine the number you have written. They are going to find out by counting the number of capitalization mistakes in a group of sentences that you have written on the board (or on handout sheets).

In your sentences, capitalize the first word of each sentence but no others, and make sure that you use words from the problematic common noun list above as well as from many of the categories in the proper noun list. When they have finished looking for mistakes and you have announced the number of mistakes they should have found, discuss the categories that have caused problems.

Answers

Page 7, Finish the Limerick
The words appear in the grid in the following order (from top to bottom): Proper: French, Easter, Tuesday, Washington, Venus, Florida, April, China; **Common:** panther, mother, summer, daffodil, teacher, biology, collie.
Limerick ending: He died in the fall.

Page 8, Answer and Question
(The number of errors appears in parentheses.)
1. Six Scottish sailors sailed the sea searching for sardines and seashells. (5) **2.** The grateful Greek girl got a gift of a groundhog on Groundhog Day. (4) **3.** On Tuesday and Thursday I test the taste of tea from Tibet and Thailand. (2) **4.** From March to May we moved from Maine to Mexico using many marvelous motorcycles. (3) **5.** I asked Kathy from Kansas to cuddle my cute koala. (3) **6.** The Jewish juggler from Jerusalem juggled Jamaican jars. (2) **7.** Does Harold, the happy Hawaiian, have helpers when he handles Henry, his huge hippopotamus? (4) **8.** Some platinum from the planet Pluto pleased playful Pauline. (3) **9.** My mother loves mathematics, Martians, marshmallows, mules, and Matilda, my aunt from Maryland. (5) **10.** On Wednesdays Wendy from Walla Walla, Washington, walks to work in her wide walking shoes. (4) **Total errors and answer to question:** 35. **Question:** In the United States, how old must you be in order to be president? **Words in line that need to be capitalized:** Paris, Russia, England, Saturn, Italy, Denmark, Egypt, November, Tuesday.

Page 9, Maze
The correct path goes through: **1.** Saturday
2. ocean **3.** Friday **4.** river **5.** nurse
6. zebra **7.** Irish **8.** Texas **9.** elephant
10. October **11.** autumn **12.** Australia
13. Mexico **14.** spring **15.** moon **16.** Latin
17. June **18.** capitalization **19.** Mars
20. waltz **21.** guitar **22.** strawberry
23. Navaho **24.** Christmas **25.** holiday
26. freshman **27.** poodle. **Bonus:** 36
Also: doctor, lion, Venus, school, professor, island, Japanese, Saturn, Easter.

Punctuation Puzzles & Mazes • Scholastic Professional Books

READY-TO-GO REPRODUCIBLES

Name _____ **Date** _____

Finish the Limerick

There once was a man named Hall,
Who fell in a spring in the fall.
'Twould have been a sad thing
If he died in the spring,
But he didn't. . . .

Directions: Finish this limerick by identifying words in the box below that are proper nouns or adjectives and those that are common. Insert the words from the box into the correct grid spaces below—proper or common. Each word should fill the spaces of one line in the grid exactly. The final line of the limerick will appear in the vertical boxes of the grid.

PROPER NOUNS

COMMON NOUNS

april
biology
china
collie
daffodil
easter
florida
french
mother
panther
summer
teacher
tuesday
venus
washington

Name _____   **Date** _____

Answer and Question

Section 1: The Answer

Directions: Correct the capitalization mistakes and write the number of corrections you make for each sentence on the line at the end. Add up the total number of corrections you made. The sum of these numbers will answer the question at the bottom of the page.

1. Six scottish Sailors sailed the Sea searching for Sardines and Seashells.   ____

2. The grateful greek girl got a gift of a Groundhog on groundhog's day.   ____

3. On tuesday and Thursday I test the taste of tea from tibet and Thailand.   ____

4. From march to May we moved from Maine to mexico using many marvelous Motorcycles.   ____

5. I asked kathy from kansas to cuddle my cute Koala.   ____

6. The jewish juggler from Jerusalem juggled jamaican jars.   ____

7. Does harold, the happy hawaiian, have helpers when he handles henry, his huge Hippopotamus?   ____

8. Some Platinum from the Planet pluto pleased playful Pauline.   ____

9. My Mother loves Mathematics, martians, marshmallows, Mules, and Matilda, my aunt from maryland.   ____

10. On wednesdays Wendy from walla walla, washington, walks to work in her wide walking shoes.   ____

Total: ____

Section 2: The Question

In the United States, how old must you be in order to be _____?

Directions: To complete the question, you must "decode" the following very long word. If you look carefully you'll see that it is really many words—common and proper nouns—that run together. Circle the first letter of each proper noun. When you have found all nine proper nouns, put the letters together to spell out the last word of the question above. The first letter has been circled for you.

waterparisdogrussiaenglandwinterprofessorsaturnitalyboxer

denmarkspringegyptnovemberhistoryeagletuesday

Punctuation Puzzles & Mazes • Scholastic Professional Books

Name _____   **Date** _____

Maze

Directions: Trace a path to the end of this maze by passing through 27 correctly capitalized common and proper nouns. Avoid all words with capitalization errors!

★ **Bonus:** How many correctly capitalized words are there in the entire maze? _____

Unit 2: Common and Proper Nouns

My first school was called Quaint School and was on a quaint street named First street.

This unit helps students decide when words that are not usually capitalized should be capitalized and when they should remain lowercase.

Rule: *Common nouns* and *adjectives* become *proper nouns* and *adjectives* when they are used as all or part of a name or a title. The context determines when common nouns and adjectives need to be capitalized.

> **Example:** The town's main street is named Main Street.

Teaching Tips

★ Students usually have no trouble capitalizing nouns and adjectives in names like Doctor Gonzales or Ivory Soap. They very often, however, forget that the last word in the names of schools, streets, hotels, and theaters must also be capitalized—*Fleabag Hotel, Saint Charles School, Main Street.*

★ Directions—*north, south, east, west*—also cause frequent errors, probably because they should be capitalized when used as the name of a particular region: *States in the West are very large.* Similarly, the names of school subjects are often incorrectly capitalized because of their frequent use in titles of particular classes: *I am taking an algebra course called Advanced Algebra.*

★ Younger students also have a hard time knowing when to capitalize the names of family members. Correct examples: *My favorite aunt is Aunt Betty. "Mom, are Dad's mom and dad coming over for dinner?"*

Punctuation Puzzles & Mazes • Scholastic Professional Books

Mini-Lesson

Capitalization in English gets very hazy (and frustrating!) at times because almost every word can be turned into a proper noun or adjective by making it a part of a name or title. Students must simply learn to notice whether they are dealing with a proper or a common noun or adjective, even if the word or words in question are almost never capitalized—*The Lost Gold Mine*, for example.

The following exercise emphasizes how word status can switch from common to proper. (This exercise can be done orally with the whole group or individually in writing.) Put a short list of words on the board and ask your students to make up two sentences for each word, one in which the word is used as a common noun or adjective and another in which it is used as a proper noun or adjective. (If they can use both forms in only one sentence, as is done in the cartoon on page 10, so much the better.)

Make most of your words relatively obvious—*library, motel, south*—but also throw in some harder ones—*yellow, horse, dandelion*. Make sure that they capitalize all the proper nouns and adjectives in their sentences, not just the ones you write on the board. If, for example, they use *dandelion* as part of the name of a school, it is likely that some of them will forget that they must also capitalize the word *school*: *I go to the Dandelion School*.

Answers

Page 12, Hidden Message
Corrected sentences: 1. In my state in the Midwest, a town named Grant is due north of a city named Lee. **2.** I never used to like seeing a doctor until I met Doctor Christos, who has an office on Beacon Street near the Stopwatch Supermarket. **3.** On my street we have two schools, a factory, and a branch office of the First National Bank. **4.** At Carver High School I'm studying history, English, mathematics, and a special course called Neighborhood Ecology. **5.** In my small town there are people of many different religions and nationalities, including Scots who are Christians, Iranians who are Muslims, Russians who are Jews, and Indians who are Hindus. **6.** Mr. Thomas, our science teacher, took the whole sophomore class to Crooked Creek to study fossils and rocks. **7.** The Karloff Theater on Fifth Street shows such scary movies that my mother won't take me there, but my aunt will.
Word on tablecloth: HAT

Page 14, Maze
The correct path goes through: 1. We went to the beach when we were in Algeria and swam in the sea. **2.** The desert is vast. **3.** The Sahara Desert extends into Mauritania. **4.** I told my friend to meet me at the Mali Cafe. **5.** This cafe has good food. **6.** Is Nigeria named after the Niger River? **7.** They speak French here. **8.** This street is Ubangi Street. **9.** In Sudan I had several professors who taught me the history of Islam. **10.** I was instructed by Professor Selassie about Ethiopian history. **11.** My hotel is very nice. **12.** In Kenya there are many lions. **13.** You can see Lake Victoria in Tanzania. **14.** Are there hippos in Zambia? **15.** Is there a doctor with an office on this street? **16.** I'm staying at Namibia Hotel in the capital, Windhoek. **17.** South Africa is as far south as you can go in Africa.
Bonus: 18 **Also:** The Mediterranean Sea is north of Libya.

Name _____   **Date** _____

Hidden Message: Huckle-Buckle Beanstalk!

A group of friends—Ramon, Miranda, Makoto, and Priscilla—are playing a game called Huckle-Buckle Beanstalk. While the others keep their eyes closed tight, Ramon hides a small object—a thimble—somewhere in the room. Locate the hidden thimble by completing the following exercise.

Directions: Find each capitalization mistake on page 13 and correct it. Shade in the grid square that matches the letter–number coordinates under each mistake. When you are done, a word will appear on the tablecloth that tells you where the thimble is. The first mistake has been corrected for you.

Huckle-Buckle Beanstalk Rules

1. One player hides a small object in plain sight.

2. The first person to find the object doesn't cry out or point it out to the others but instead pretends not to see it and moves somewhere else in the room before calling out, "Huckle-buckle beanstalk!"

3. That person gets to hide the object the next time—after the others have all found it.

Punctuation Puzzles & Mazes • Scholastic Professional Books

Name _____ **Date** _____

Hidden Message: Huckle-Buckle Beanstalk!

1. In my State in the Midwest, a town named grant is due North of a City named Lee.
       ‾‾   ‾‾‾‾‾‾‾   ‾‾‾‾‾   ‾‾‾‾‾   ‾‾‾‾   ‾‾‾
       J4   D2   A6   G2   E5   L3

2. I never used to like seeing a Doctor until I met Doctor Christos, who has an Office on
                                  ‾‾‾‾‾‾   ‾‾‾‾‾‾ ‾‾‾‾‾‾‾‾   ‾‾‾‾‾‾
                                  I2   L6   H4   E3

   Beacon street near the Stopwatch supermarket.
          ‾‾‾‾‾‾   ‾‾‾‾‾‾‾‾‾
          J6   F1   C5

3. On my Street we have two Schools, a factory, and a branch Office of the First
         ‾‾‾‾‾‾   ‾‾‾‾‾‾‾   ‾‾‾‾‾‾   ‾‾‾‾‾
         A2   G6   K4   D4   A4   B2

   National bank.
   ‾‾‾‾‾‾‾‾ ‾‾‾‾
   H6   C2

4. At Carver high school I'm studying History, english, mathematics, and a special
         ‾‾‾‾‾‾ ‾‾‾‾ ‾‾‾‾‾‾   ‾‾‾‾‾‾‾‾ ‾‾‾‾‾‾‾ ‾‾‾‾‾‾‾‾‾‾‾
         L1   G4   C3   J5   E6   D3

   course called Neighborhood ecology.
   ‾‾‾‾‾‾   ‾‾‾‾‾‾‾‾‾‾‾‾ ‾‾‾‾‾‾‾
   I5   B5   G5

5. In my small Town there are people of many different religions and Nationalities,
                  ‾‾‾‾‾‾   ‾‾‾‾‾‾‾‾   ‾‾‾‾‾‾‾‾‾‾‾‾‾
                  C6   B3   A5

   including Scots who are christians, iranians who are Muslims, russians who are jews,
            ‾‾‾‾‾   ‾‾‾‾‾‾‾‾‾‾ ‾‾‾‾‾‾‾‾   ‾‾‾‾‾‾‾ ‾‾‾‾‾‾‾‾   ‾‾‾‾
            J1   E2   J3   L4   A3   E4

   and indians who are Hindus.
       ‾‾‾‾‾‾‾   ‾‾‾‾‾‾
       G3   B6

6. Mr. Thomas, our Science teacher, took the whole sophomore class to Crooked creek
       ‾‾‾ ‾‾‾‾‾‾   ‾‾‾‾‾‾‾ ‾‾‾‾‾‾‾   ‾‾‾‾‾‾‾‾ ‾‾‾‾‾   ‾‾‾‾‾‾‾ ‾‾‾‾‾
       H3 C4   F5   I1   D6   K5   F4

   to study fossils and rocks.

7. The Karloff theater on Fifth street shows such scary Movies that my Mother won't
          ‾‾‾‾‾‾‾ ‾‾‾‾‾‾‾   ‾‾‾‾‾ ‾‾‾‾‾‾   ‾‾‾‾‾‾   ‾‾‾‾‾‾
          A1   J2   I6   F2   K2   B4

   take me there, but my aunt will.
                           ‾‾‾‾
                           K6

Common and Proper Nouns

Name _____ Date _____

Maze

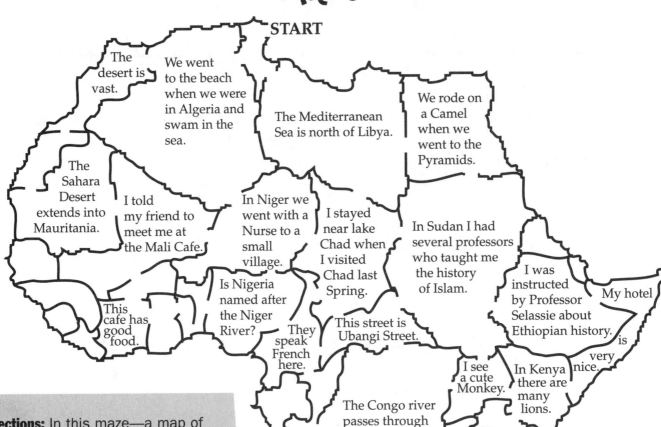

START

The desert is vast.

We went to the beach when we were in Algeria and swam in the sea.

The Mediterranean Sea is north of Libya.

We rode on a Camel when we went to the Pyramids.

The Sahara Desert extends into Mauritania.

I told my friend to meet me at the Mali Cafe.

In Niger we went with a Nurse to a small village.

I stayed near lake Chad when I visited Chad last Spring.

In Sudan I had several professors who taught me the history of Islam.

I was instructed by Professor Selassie about Ethiopian history.

My hotel is very nice.

Is Nigeria named after the Niger River?

This cafe has good food.

They speak French here.

This street is Ubangi Street.

I see a cute Monkey.

In Kenya there are many lions.

The Congo river passes through Zaire.

You can see Lake Victoria in Tanzania.

In April it's Fall here.

Is there a doctor with an office on this street?

Are there hippos in Zambia?

END

I'm staying at Namibia Hotel in the capital, Windhoek.

Are we looking West or East?

South Africa is as far south as you can go in Africa.

Directions: In this maze—a map of Africa—travel from the start (Tunisia) to the end (Zimbabwe) by tracing a path through countries with sentences that contain only correct capitalization. You may pass through the borders of any country that is too small to contain a sentence. The correct path passes through 17 sentences with correct capitalization.

★ **Bonus:** How many correct sentences are there in the entire maze? _____

Punctuation Puzzles & Mazes • Scholastic Professional Books

Unit 3: Sentence Fragments

Units 3, 4, and 5 provide strategies for and practice with identifying complete sentences and fixing the most common sentence problems: fragments and run-ons. Unit 3 focuses on identifying and correcting sentence fragments.

It is often difficult to spot sentence fragments. Especially when they seem connected to the preceding sentence.

Definition: *Sentence fragments* are incomplete thoughts that have been punctuated as if they were sentences.

Example: A sentence like this one, for example.

Teaching Tips

★ Students often find it difficult to recognize fragments and thus to eliminate them from their writing. Why? They are assailed with fragments every day—when they think, when they converse, when they write dialogue, and even when they read.

Expert writers use fragments to fit their style and the occasion. If students are to use fragments effectively in their writing, then first they need to be able to distinguish between fragments and complete thoughts.

★ The example above illustrates the most common fragment error: An incomplete thought that is really an extension of a preceding thought is punctuated as if it were a separate sentence. These mistakes often occur in explanations and examples.

The easiest way to correct this kind of error is simply to attach the offending fragment to the sentence before it by removing the preceding period, adding a comma (if necessary) and changing the uppercase letter to lowercase. Alternatively, you can turn the fragment into a sentence by adding a subject or other needed words.

Sentence with fragment: I always admired Gandhi. The great Indian leader.

Correction: I always admired Gandhi, the great Indian leader.

Alternative: I always admired Gandhi. He was a great Indian leader.

★ Students also can be reassured that fragments in quoted dialogue are perfectly correct since we so often leave out words when we speak.

Mini-Lesson

Since students experience the most trouble identifying sentence fragments when the fragments are combined with a related thought, exercises should include the complete thoughts that set up and mask the fragments as well as the fragments themselves.

Sentence Fragments

To get your students used to proofreading for fragments, write some of the common patterns on the board—complete thoughts followed by fragments that are examples, explanations, and other related phrases—and then ask for ideas about how to correct each one. Some students will want to add words to make the fragment a separate sentence while most will probably want to attach it to the preceding thought. Go through the appropriate punctuation changes. In some cases no punctuation may be needed, in some a comma will need to be inserted in place of the period, and for lists or examples you may need a dash or colon.

Here are a few examples and possible corrections:

Example: These are the contenders. Martha, Maya, and Frances.

Correction: These are the contenders: Martha, Maya, and Frances.

Example: He was lost in his own world. Dreaming of daring deeds in distant lands.

Correction: He was lost in his own world, dreaming of daring deeds in distant lands.

Example: We'll get lunch. After we do our shopping.

Correction: We'll get lunch after we do our shopping.

Example: You will enjoy the performance. But not for long!

Correction: You will enjoy the performance—but not for long!

Answers

Page 17, Message in a Grid
Fragments: 2, 5, 6, 8, 9, 12. **Answer:** Russia

Page 18, Maze
Answer Key: The correct path goes through: **1.** My aunt has a bright red umbrella. **2.** A strong wind broke my umbrella. **3.** Umbrellas have a long, interesting history. **4.** Will it rain tonight? **5.** My umbrella didn't keep my feet dry! **6.** A few lightning bolts are sixty miles long. **7.** I love to hear rain on the roof. **8.** Didn't you wear your boots? **9.** I always lose my umbrellas. **10.** Do you know what to do in a thunderstorm? **11.** The weather is often hard to predict.
Bonus: 1. Umbrellas used as sunshades are called *parasols*. **2.** The Romans used parasols.

Punctuation Puzzles & Mazes • Scholastic Professional Books

READY-TO-GO REPRODUCIBLES

Name _____   **Date** _____

Message in a Grid

What is the largest country in the world? _____

Directions: Find the answer to this question in the grid below by correctly identifying the sentence fragments in the following exercise. Circle the number of any example that is a fragment. Then, circle the letter in the grid that matches. The first fragment has been identified for you.

1. Jacqueline loved her dog.

2. A Great Dane named Raina who was almost a perfect pet.

3. Raina was playful, loving, gentle, smart, and obedient (usually).

4. She did, however, have one or two bad habits.

5. Like getting too excited sometimes when Jacqueline took her for a walk on her leash.

6. Which made Jacqueline think that she was holding back a horse rather than a dog.

7. You see, Raina weighed over 140 pounds.

8. And was almost four feet tall and very powerful.

9. Making her very hard to restrain if she saw another dog, a squirrel, or some other small animal.

10. What did Jacqueline do in such a situation?

11. She spoke to Raina in a serious, commanding voice.

12. And then looked for a tree, a park bench, or something else very solid that she could hold on to for dear life!

3	2	7	4	12	10	6	11	9	5	1	8
B	R	E	A	U	Z	S	M	S	I	L	A

Name _____   **Date** _____

Maze

Directions: Trace a path from start to finish that passes through 11 complete sentences. Avoid sentence fragments, for they act as blocks!

A chance of showers today.

Sunny and warm tomorrow.

The weather is often hard to predict.

Do you know what to do in a thunderstorm?

Dark clouds, making rain seem very likely.

My grandmother's parasol made of silk.

I always lose my umbrellas.

Not much good in a hurricane.

Three people under one umbrella.

A mixture of rain, sleet, and very wet snow.

Lightning often striking tall buildings.

Didn't you wear your boots?

I love to hear rain on the roof.

Rain not stopping the football game.

Most lightning staying within clouds.

A few lightning bolts are sixty miles long.

My umbrella didn't keep my feet dry!

Umbrella, from the Latin *umbra*, meaning shade.

END

The Romans used parasols.

Umbrellas have a long, interesting history.

Will it rain tonight?

A strong wind broke my umbrella.

Bending it inside out in one big gust.

START

My aunt has a bright red umbrella.

Umbrellas used as sunshades are called *parasols*.

★ **Bonus:** Can you find two more complete sentences that are not on the correct path to the end?

_____

_____

18

READY·TO·GO REPRODUCIBLES

Unit 4: Identifying Run-On Sentences

The exercises in this unit ask students to identify run-on sentences and recognize that two thoughts joined by a coordinating conjunction form a complete sentence.

Definition: A *run-on sentence* runs two or more independent clauses together as if they were only one clause. The most frequent form of run-on sentence is the *comma splice*, which occurs when the complete thoughts are separated with a comma rather than a period or semicolon.

Run-ons need frequent attention, they cause chronic punctuation problems.

I agree I sometimes don't spot run-ons myself.

Examples:

Run-on sentence: This is a run-on sentence it has two complete thoughts that are run together.

Correction with a period: This was a run-on sentence. It had two complete thoughts that were run together.

Run-on sentence: Comma splices have some punctuation, however, a comma isn't sufficient.

Correction with a semicolon: Comma splices have some punctuation; however, a comma isn't sufficient.

Teaching Tips

★ A common misconception is that run-on sentences are lengthy, running on and on. In fact, many run-on sentences are quite short—as short as two words. In this run-on, two commands are joined incorrectly with a comma: *Look, run!* The most frequent run-on errors combine two such closely related brief thoughts.

★ A second misconception is that the use of linking expressions, like *however*, *in fact*, *therefore*, *actually*, *for example*, and *for instance*, allow complete thoughts to be joined with a comma, as in the second example above. If you move the adverb *however* to the end of the sentence, you can see more easily that it is a run-on: *Comma splices have some punctuation, a comma isn't sufficient, however.*

☀ There are six words that do allow complete thoughts to be joined with a comma. They are the coordinating conjunctions *and*, *but*, *or*, *nor*, *for*, and *yet*.

These conjunctions can only connect two sentences at the beginning of the second complete thought, and they are correctly used to join two ideas with a comma: *Comma splices are common, but they can be avoided by using a coordinating conjunction*.

Mini-Lesson

Mix up run-ons with correctly punctuated sentences and write these examples on the board. Have students identify the incorrect punctuation by asking themselves if both parts of the sentence are complete thoughts. Here's an alternating series of run-on and complete-sentence examples.

Run-on: You should have seen my cat, she did something cute.

Complete Sentence: She was chasing a butterfly, and the butterfly seemed to play with her.

Run-on: It flew up high, then it came down behind her.

Complete Sentence: She spun around, her tail twitching and her ears pinned back.

Run-on: The butterfly seemed to tease her, in fact, it landed on her tail.

Complete Sentence: Even though I had my camera, I could never get in position to take a photo.

Run-on: I wish I'd had a video camera, a TV station might have shown a tape of my cat with that butterfly.

Answers

Page 21, Treasure Hunt
The correct clues, in order, are: **1.** The next clue is by the shovels; go at your own risk. **2.** You found the shovels, but now you must choose a clue on a barn. **3.** If this clue is correct, you should find a cat. **4.** You've come far, but you still must choose one of the clues under the fence. **5.** Success could be near, and a clover might bring you some good luck. **6.** The treasure is at hand; just look under a hat. **7.** You've found the treasure; a clear understanding of how to avoid run-ons is as good as gold.

Page 22, Dialogue Mystery
All are run-on sentences except the following: (10) I can't find my glasses, and I know I left them on the desk! (11) I'm glad you're here, but why are you laughing? (8) Did you go to the kitchen sink to clean them, or did you stay here in the living room? (1) Sarah, you're laughing again! You're making her angry! **Solution:** She has them on.

Page 23, Maze
The correct path goes through: **1.** I hope that you enjoy challenges, for this maze requires skill, knowledge, and careful, patient work. **2.** It was a dark and stormy night, but I was happy because I was reading a mystery. **3.** A synonym for *maze* is *labyrinth*, a word that came to English from Ancient Greek. **4.** I'm feeling insecure about this path, but maybe I should persist. **5.** I'm not sure why, but mazes make me dizzy. **6.** I could have worked backwards, but I didn't.
Bonus: 9 **Also: 1.** Some people love meat; some love vegetables. **2.** Four-leafed clovers are supposed to bring good luck, and so are horseshoes, charms, and amulets. **3.** After a long day of hard work I take a hot bath, for baths usually relax me.

Name _____ **Date** _____

Treasure Hunt

Directions: To find the treasure start at the top and follow the clues that are correctly punctuated. Trace a path as you go, avoiding all clues that contain run-on sentences.

Begin here by choosing one of the three messages below, and be careful to avoid run-on sentences.

The treasure is nearby, you just need to find a cone to get going.

The next clue is by the shovels; dig at your own risk.

Go to the tree, read the message you find there.

Find a dog, then you'll know much more.

This could be the right clue, if so, go to the dog.

If this clue is correct, you should find a cat.

The bag contains fool's gold, you must start over.

You've earned the treasure; a clear understanding of how to avoid run-ons is as good as gold.

The treasure is at hand; just look under a hat.

There are more clues to find, the next one is under a tombstone.

You've come far, but you still must choose one of the clues under the fence.

The treasure may be yours, you just need to find a bag of gold coins.

Success could be near, and a clover might bring you some good luck.

Go back to the start, you've missed two run-on sentences.

You've made some errors, now you get to start over.

You found the shovels, but now you must choose one of the clues on a barn.

Identifying Run-On Sentences

Name _____   Date _____

Dialogue Mystery

Directions: Solve the mystery of the disappearing glasses by identifying the run-on sentences in the dialogue. Circle the underlined letter in each incorrectly punctuated sentence. (There are 12 in all.) Then, write each circled letter in the answer space that matches the number at the end of the sentence. An example has been given.

Answer:

$$\frac{\quad}{1} \ \frac{\quad}{2} \ \frac{\quad}{3} \quad \frac{\quad}{4} \ \frac{\quad}{5} \ \frac{\quad}{6} \quad \frac{t}{7} \ \frac{\quad}{8} \ \frac{\quad}{9} \ \frac{\quad}{10} \quad \frac{\quad}{11} \ \frac{\quad}{12}.$$

Example: Sarah and Ben Jordan were playing when they heard an angry cry, it was the voice of their mother in the next room. (7)

Sarah:	What is it, Mom, is something wrong? (4)
Ms. Jordan:	I can't find my glasses, and I know I left them on the desk! (10)
Ben:	Coming, Mom, we'll help you find them! (2)
Ms. Jordan:	I'm glad you're here, but why are you laughing? (11)
Ben:	Sorry, Mom. I'll stop, and you stop, too, Sarah. (1)
Ms. Jordan:	I saw you wink at Sarah as you said that, I don't think this is anything to laugh about! (6)
Sarah:	Okay, Mom. We'll be serious, just tell us what you were doing when you had them last. (9)
Ms. Jordan:	I took them off to clean them, then the phone rang. (11)
Ben:	Did you go to the kitchen sink to clean them, or did you stay here in the living room? (8)
Ms. Jordan:	I never left this room, it's a total mystery! (3)
Ben:	Sarah, you're laughing again, you're making her angry! (1)
Sarah:	Mom, don't be mad, I'm just laughing because I know how happy you'll feel when you find your glasses. (10)
Ben:	And I have a feeling that you're going to find them very soon, maybe Sarah can give you a hint. (8)
Sarah:	Okay, Mom, here's your hint, I'm looking right at them! (5)
Ms. Jordan:	Oh, now I see why you were laughing, I've finally found them! (12)

Punctuation Puzzles & Mazes • Scholastic Professional Books

Name _____   **Date** _____

Maze

Directions: Find the path to the finish that passes through six correctly punctuated sentences. Avoid all run-ons!

★ **Bonus:** How many correctly punctuated sentences are there in the entire maze? _____

Four-leafed clovers are supposed to bring good luck, and so are horseshoes, charms, and amulets.

After a long day of hard work I take a hot bath, for baths usually relax me.

I need to relax right now, this maze is driving me crazy!

It's almost time for bed, I'm not tired at all.

I'll go right through here, then I'll be home.

Shortcuts can sometimes cause problems, in fact, it would often be more accurate to call them longcuts.

Solving easy problems is satisfying, solving difficult ones is even more gratifying.

Some mazes are very clever and original, they truly amaze me!

I could have worked backwards, but I didn't.

I thought I was right, however, I was not.

because I was reading a mystery.

knowledge, and careful, patient work.

some love vegetables.

Some people love meat;

Kids are always teased for having their hair cut, I wonder why.

happy, but I was happy

It was a dark and stormy night, but I

for this maze requires skill,

Punctuation Puzzles & Mazes • Scholastic Professional Books

This is my night to do the dishes there aren't many.

I hope that you enjoy challenges, for this maze can go straight.

it came from Ancient Greek.

but mazes make me dizzy.

Many run-on sentences are long, some are very short.

The shortest distance between two points is a straight line.

A synonym for *maze* is labyrinth, a word that came to English from Ancient Greek.

I'm feeling insecure about this path, but maybe I should persist.

I'm not sure why, but mazes make me dizzy.

in mazes you rarely can go straight.

FINISH

START

Unit 5: Correcting Run-On Sentences

Subordinating conjunctions correct run-on sentences *when*

they are inserted before one of the complete thoughts.

The exercises in Unit 5 focus on correcting run-on sentences with subordinating conjunctions. This method encourages students to write complex sentences rather than simply recast the run-on as two simple sentences or one compound sentence.

Definition: Subordinating conjunctions take a complete thought and make it part of another complete thought. They include words such as *when*, *if*, *while*, *as*, and *though* that show the relationship between the two ideas they connect.

Examples:

Complete thought: he is so tall

Incomplete thought (subordinating conjunction added): *because* he is so tall

Run-on sentence corrected with *because*: I'm sure to see him ^*because* he is so tall.

Teaching Tips

★ Young writers often have a choppy style because they express most of their ideas as simple sentences (sentences with only one complete thought) or as compound sentences (sentences with two complete thoughts, usually connected with the coordinating conjunctions *and* or *but*). When they begin to replace *and* and *but* with more specific subordinating conjunctions—such as *after*, *as*, *if*, and *although*—then their styles immediately sound more fluent and mature.

★ When students use subordinating conjunctions, they clarify and refine their writing by separating their ideas into main and secondary parts. In this compound sentence, where two complete thoughts are connected with *and*, neither idea carries more weight than the other: *Women won the right to vote in 1920, and they gained more influence in our society.* If we recast the sentence by using the subordinating conjunction *after* and delete the word *and*, the sentence now stresses the idea that women have more influence now than before achieving suffrage: After *women won the right to vote in 1920, they gained more influence in our society.*

READY·TO·GO
REPRODUCIBLES

★ If you did not use the last unit before doing this one, be sure that students don't confuse adverbs such as *however* and *therefore* with subordinating conjunctions:

Obvious run-on sentence: I like her, she doesn't like me, however.

Less obvious run-on sentence: I like her, however, she doesn't like me.

Corrected sentences with a subordinating conjunction: a) Although she doesn't like me, I like her. b) I like her even though she doesn't like me.

Mini-Lesson

It helps students to see that punctuation and grammar study can truly improve their writing. This unit shows how good punctuation goes hand in hand with a mature, graceful, and forceful style.

Under the general rubric of "sentence improvement," write a run-on sentence on the board that lends itself to several types of correction—for example, *I'm really happy, I just had some good news*. After discussing why it is a run-on sentence—specifically, a comma splice—ask for suggestions about ways to correct it. See if you can draw out a variety of solutions, from simple punctuation changes to the use of coordinating and subordinating conjunctions:

> I'm really happy. I just had some good news.
>
> I'm really happy; I just had some good news.
>
> I'm really happy, for I just had some good news.
>
> I'm really happy because I just had some good news.

Finally, ask your students which of those corrections sounds the most fluent, which style they prefer. Chances are that most students will gravitate towards the last example, finding it less choppy than the others.

Answers

Page 26, Word Find
Answers: 1. before **2.** though (although) **3.** because (since, as) **4.** as (while, when) **5.** If **6.** When (After, Before) **7.** Since (Because, If, As) **8.** Although (Though) **9.** until (before, unless) **10.** After (When) **11.** unless **12.** while (when)

Page 27, Answer in a Grid
(in the order they appear in the story)
8. because **5.** unless **13.** until **4.** if **10.** since **6.** before **9.** although **1.** as **7.** after **2.** unless **11.** though **3.** while **12.** when
Answer to riddle: You are...as wise as an owl.

Correcting Run-On Sentences

Name_____ Date _____

Word Find

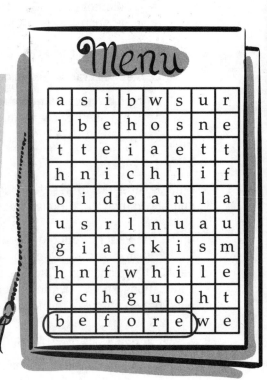

Directions: Write in the missing subordinating conjunctions in each example to join two complete thoughts. (All 12 of the words you will need can be found in the grid.) Try to use a different conjuction for each example even though there may be more than one that will fit in some examples. The first one has been done for you.

Hint: The answers in the word grid are mixed in with many other letters and run in every direction—across, backward, up and down, and diagonally.

a	s	i	b	w	s	u	r
l	b	e	h	o	s	n	e
t	t	e	i	a	e	t	t
h	n	i	c	h	l	i	f
o	i	d	e	a	n	l	a
u	s	r	l	n	u	a	u
g	i	a	c	k	i	s	m
h	n	f	w	h	i	l	e
e	c	h	g	u	o	h	t
b	e	f	o	r	e	w	e

1. The pushy waiter wanted me to order ____before____ I was finished reading the menu.

2. I think I'll have a salad _____ the clam chowder sounds good, too.

3. I am not eating meat _____ I'm a vegetarian.

4. My napkin dropped on the floor _____ I was reaching for the salt shaker.

5. _____ your steak is undercooked, you should send it back.

6. _____ this four-course meal is over, I'll certainly be full.

7. _____ you don't like sweet things, maybe we should skip dessert.

8. _____ I like ice cream, I rarely eat it.

9. I'm not going to stop eating _____ I've eaten every morsel.

10. _____ this big meal is over, I think I'll take a long walk.

11. I'll order a cup of coffee _____ you really want to go now.

12. I'll get our coats _____ the waiter is getting the check.

READY-TO-GO REPRODUCIBLES

Punctuation Puzzles & Mazes • Scholastic Professional Books

Name_____   Date _____

Answer in a Grid

Anagrams are two different words formed from the same letters.

Riddle: If you can find an anagram for the word *low*, you are

___ ___ ___ ___ ___ ___ ___ ___ ___ ___ ___ ___ ___ ___ .

Directions: Complete the exercise below to discover the rest of the riddle spelled out in the boxes of the grid. Choose the best subordinating conjunction from the answer box to substitute for each number in the story. Then write your answer on the grid line that matches the number of the correction you made. (Your answer must fit the puzzle spaces exactly.) The first one has been done for you. **Hint:** One conjunction from the box is used twice.

Subordinating Conjunctions

after	although	as
because ✓	before	if
since	though	unless
until	when	while

because

One Saturday Theo found himself alone at home (8) his father had gone shopping and his mother was helping a friend who had broken her ankle. (5) I think of something to do soon, I'm going to get bored, thought Theo.

He started thinking up and then rejecting project after project (13) finally an exciting idea popped into his head. (4) Theo had stopped to consider, he would have realized the source of his idea. (10) he had just finished a book about great explorers and treasure hunters, his idea was to explore his musty old attic.

(6) another minute had passed, Theo was climbing the attic stairs with a flashlight in his hand. (9) the attic had two naked lightbulbs hanging from the rafters, there were still many dark corners and dingy crannies full of spider webs.

(1) Theo pushed open the rarely used attic door, a musty smell filled his nostrils and a cloud of dust motes rose around his shoes. I'm going to need to shower (7) I find the treasure, he thought. He wasn't sure just what the treasure would be, (2) maybe it was some long-forgotten letter from an ancestor with a priceless stamp on it.

Unfortunately, Theo's exploration did not result in his finding anything priceless, (11) he did have an experience that he never forgot. (3) he was prying open the lid of a large, dusty trunk, his father, who had come home and heard strange noises in the attic, came up unnoticed behind him and said, "Theo, what are you doing?"

In his fright at hearing the unexpected voice, Theo leapt up and smashed his head into a low rafter. (12) his mother came home a little later, she found that she had to help another person who had been in a recent accident.

1. ___ ___ ___ ___ ___
2. ___ ___ ___ ___ ___

3. ___ ___ ___ ___ ___
4. ___ ___ ___ ___ ___
5. ___ ___ ___ ___ ___
6. ___ ___ ___ ___ ___

7. ___ ___ ___ ___ ___
8. <u>b e c a u s e</u>

9. ___ ___ ___ ___ ___ ___ ___
10. ___ ___ ___ ___

11. ___ ___ ___ ___ ___
12. ___ ___ ___ ___

13. ___ ___ ___ ___ ___

Unit 6: Items in a Series

I see sparrows, crows and robins.

Unit 6 reviews a fairly easy use of the comma—separating items in a series. Units 7, 8, and 9 provide practice for more complicated uses of the comma—setting off adjective and adverb clauses, direct addresses, unemphatic exclamations, and parenthetical expressions.

Rule 1: Commas separate three or more items of a series. These items may be as simple as a group of nouns or as complicated as a group of independent clauses. (Note: Items in a series should be of the same kind; i.e., they should be in parallel form.)

> **Examples:**   peas, carrots, and potatoes (all items are nouns)
> Punctuation is difficult, grammar is frustrating, and spelling is downright impossible. (all items are independent clauses)

Teaching Tips

★ The comma just before the conjunction in a series with three or more items is optional. Many editors—notably those at *The New York Times*—prefer to omit that last comma: *peas, carrots and potatoes*. But because the omission of that comma might suggest that the last two items are being grouped as a pair, many editors prefer to use it.

Note: The answer keys for the exercises in this unit use the optional comma, but omitting it is fine as long as you are consistent.

★ The series *peas, carrots, and potatoes* needs comma separation, but *peas and carrots* does not.

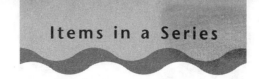
Rule 2: Commas separate two adjectives in a series if *and* could be inserted between the adjectives and the idea would stay the same.

> **Example:** the miserable, gray day (check: the miserable *and* gray day)

★ Notice that a comma is needed for the *large, friendly dog* but not when a coordinating conjunction is added, as in *the large but friendly dog.* Nor is a comma needed if a conjunction could not be inserted between the adjectives—e.g., *the little old man.*

Note: The first exercise does not require decisions about the separation of two adjectives in a series, and the second exercise has only a few easy ones. The third exercise, however, asks students to make several decisions about the need for a comma between two adjectives.

Mini-Lesson

Students remember to use the punctuation rules they've learned when they apply them immediately in their own writing—the sooner, the better. It is a good idea, then, to have students themselves write sentences for their classmates to punctuate.

One way to do this is to write a list of categories on the board (vegetables, sports, cities, colors, cars, and so on) and assign each student, or have each one choose, a category. Then ask all of them to write several sentences that use series of items from their categories, sometimes using only two items and sometimes using three or more. See if they can make at least one of their sentences more complex by making their series a list of phrases or clauses rather than single items.

Finally, have them punctuate each other's sentences, either by going around the class and having each student read a sentence aloud for another student to punctuate orally or by having each of them exchange papers with another student.

Answers

Page 30, What's Wrong With This Picture?
Corrected sentences that need commas (the comma before the conjunction is optional): 1. Aren't you glad that the coyotes, moose, and bears stayed home? **2.** Let's run home, make a sign, and see if we can join them. **3.** Take one sip, and you'll shake, rattle, and roll!
4. Stop trapping, poisoning, and screaming at us! **5.** Speak out against fleas, ticks, and loose dogs! **6.** Dogs should not be left alone, beaten, or locked in cars!
Sentences that should not have commas:
1. I guess that mice have to eat and keep warm like the rest of us. **2.** Want the music that's both hot and cool? **3.** Water pistols: a refreshing and fun way to hunt! **4.** No more milk or cream if we don't get better food!

Page 32, Maze
1. Pyramids are found in Egypt and in Central America. **2.** This pyramid is dark, dank, musty, and frightening. **3.** Is this a passage, a room, or a dead end? **4.** Watch out for booby traps and falling stones! **5.** I brought extra batteries, candles, water, and food. **6.** At least we haven't seen any rats or scorpions yet. **7.** The walls are rough, mossy, and damp. **8.** I've never been afraid of small, dark, airless places—until now. **9.** Who told us that exploring pyramids is easy, fun, and rewarding? **10.** I can't say how far we've gone, what level we're on, or which way is out. **11.** My watch and my voice recorder both just stopped working. **12.** First I could stand upright, then I had to stoop, and now I have to crawl. **13.** Do you think we should give up and try to find our way out? **14.** Should we go down this hole, up the ladder, or through the crack in the wall? **15.** I wish we had a cell phone, a radio, or an emergency line to contact people. **16.** There are strange, eerie, and upsetting echoes when we talk and walk. **17.** My heart is racing, my palms are sweating, and my teeth are chattering. **18.** I think I see golden statues, ancient dishes, and a mummy case.

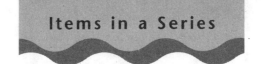

Name_____ **Date** _____

What's Wrong With This Picture?

Treeville is a sleepy little town in the north near mountains and forests. Imagine how surprised its residents were when they found themselves in the midst of a political demonstration—by animals!

In this picture you'll see what the animals were protesting. You'll also see, if you look carefully, that some animals don't know the rule for using commas to separate the items of a series. And maybe some of the humans don't either!

Directions: Find the punctuation errors in the signs and dialogue. Then rewrite the sentences correctly in the spaces provided. (You should be able to find six sentences that are missing commas and four that have commas but shouldn't.)

Corrections

Sentences that need commas:

1. _____

2. _____

3. _____

4. _____

5. _____

6. _____

Sentences that should not have commas:

1. _____

2. _____

3. _____

4. _____

Punctuation Puzzles & Mazes • Scholastic Professional Books

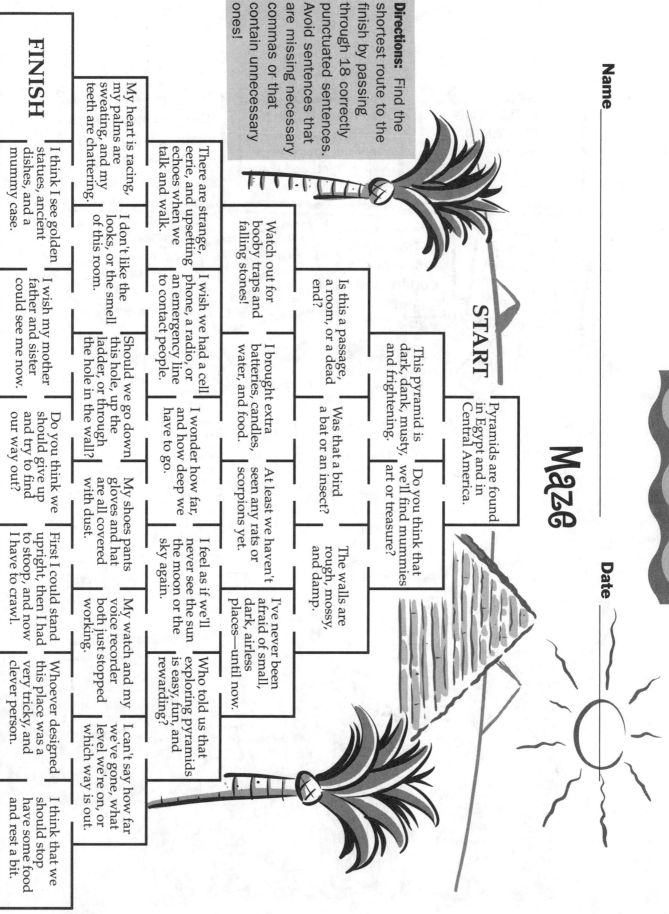

Maze

Directions: Find the shortest route to the finish by passing through 18 correctly punctuated sentences. Avoid sentences that are missing necessary commas or that contain unnecessary ones!

START

Pyramids are found in Egypt and in Central America.

This pyramid is dark, dank, musty, and frightening.

Do you think that we'll find mummies art or treasure?

Is this a passage, a room, or a dead end?

Was that a bird a bat or an insect?

The walls are rough, mossy, and damp.

Watch out for booby traps and falling stones!

I brought extra batteries, candles, water, and food.

At least we haven't seen any rats or scorpions yet.

I've never been afraid of small, dark, airless places—until now.

There are strange, eerie, and upsetting echoes when we talk and walk.

I wish we had a cell phone, a radio, or an emergency line to contact people.

I wonder how far, and how deep we have to go.

I feel as if we'll never see the sun the moon or the sky again.

Who told us that exploring pyramids is easy, fun, and rewarding?

I don't like the looks, or the smell of this room.

Should we go down this hole, up the ladder, or through the hole in the wall?

My shoes pants gloves and hat are all covered with dust.

My watch and my voice recorder both just stopped working.

I can't say how far we've gone, what level we're on, or which way is out.

My heart is racing, my palms are sweating, and my teeth are chattering.

I think I see golden statues, ancient dishes, and a mummy case.

I wish my mother father and sister could see me now.

Do you think we should give up and try to find our way out?

First I could stand upright, then I had to stoop, and now I have to crawl.

Whoever designed this place was a very tricky, and clever person.

I think that we should stop have some food and rest a bit.

FINISH

Unit 7: Adjective Clauses

Adjective clauses that are essential elements are not set off with commas.

Nonessential adjective clauses, which are sometimes called nonrestrictive clauses, are set off with commas.

This unit focuses on *adjective clauses*, related groups of words with a subject and verb that are usually placed immediately after the noun or pronoun they modify. The exercises help students to identify and properly set off these adjective clauses with commas.

Definition: A *clause* is a group of related words that has a subject and a verb. An *adjective clause* is a clause that modifies a noun or a pronoun and usually begins with one of the relative pronouns *who*, *which*, or *that*. (Sometimes the pronoun is implied but not stated. See Rule 1, second example, below.)

Rule 1: Take the adjective clause out of the sentence. If the sentence doesn't make sense without it, keep the clause without adding commas. (This is called an *essential* or *restrictive* clause.)

Examples: This is the only book *that I can recommend*.
(adjective clause beginning with the relative pronoun *that*)

This is the only book *I can recommend*.
(adjective clause with an implied relative pronoun)

Rule 2: Take the adjective clause out of the sentence. If the sentence makes sense without it, add commas to set off the clause. (This is called a *nonessential* or *nonrestrictive* clause.)

Examples: I gave the book to Sabrina, who always loves mysteries.

I hated the movie "Jaws," which gave me nightmares for a week.

Teaching Tip

★ Students often ask when they should use the relative pronouns *which* and *that*. Over the centuries the two have often been used interchangeably, but many writers follow this procedure: Use *which* to introduce nonrestrictive clauses (when you need commas) and *that* to introduce restrictive clauses (when no commas are needed).

Examples: Hurried students often skip breakfast, *which* is my favorite meal.

The meal *that* I like best is breakfast.

Punctuation Puzzles & Mazes • Scholastic Professional Books

Adjective Clauses

Mini-Lesson

In order to punctuate adjective clauses correctly students first must be able to recognize these clauses and, second, to understand the difference between essential (restrictive) and nonessential (nonrestrictive) ones. You can address both of these needs by writing on the board unpunctuated pairs of sentences that have the same adjective clauses. However, one clause in each pair must give essential information and the other must give nonessential information.

Example:

Anyone who is ready to go can get on the bus.

Luca who is ready to go can get on the bus.
(correction: Luca, who is ready to go, can get on the bus.)

The third problem which caused me the most trouble was supposed to be the easiest on the test.
(correction: The third problem, which caused me the most trouble, was supposed to be the easiest on the test.)

The problem that caused me the most trouble on the test was the third one.

First ask the students to pick out the adjective clauses in each pair and then ask which sentences need commas. Let this generate a discussion of why one clause in each pair needs to be set off with commas while the other does not. You don't even need to use the grammatical terms *restrictive* and *nonrestrictive* as long as the idea is understood: A clause with essential information should not be set off with commas, but a clause with nonessential information must be.

Answers

Page 35, What's Wrong With This Picture?
Corrected sentences: Signs: 1. Sculptures in this area that are made of marble may be touched lightly. **2.** Picasso, who was Spanish, lived most of his life in France. **Students: 1.** The paintings that I like best are the watercolors. **2.** Anyone who paints with those colors must be color blind! **3.** I like paintings that are realistic. **4.** This painting, which the guard said was very valuable, looks upside down to me. **5.** The woman who painted this is from China. **Guard:** The paintings in this room, which are all by twentieth-century artists, are recent acquisitions.

Page 36, Maze
The correct path to the end goes through: 1. Shoes, which are made in many different ways, protect our feet. **2.** Shoes that need frequent polishing can be a chore. **3.** Ballet dancers, whose feet often get hurt, wear only soft slippers. **4.** Shoes that don't fit are bad for your feet. **5.** Trish, whose shoes are untied, might trip. **6.** People who stand all day need special shoes. **7.** Dianne, who always likes to be comfortable, loves to wear loafers.
Bonus: 10 **Also: 8.** People who embark on a long journey need comfortable shoes. **9.** My father, who loves clothes, has ten pairs of shoes. **10.** The sandals that I just bought are cool.

READY-TO-GO REPRODUCIBLES

Name_____ **Date** _____

What's Wrong With This Picture?

The seventh grade at the Evers School is visiting an art museum....Do you notice anything wrong with this picture of their visit?

Directions: Find and correct all the comma errors in the signs and the dialogue.
Hint: Sometimes you must add commas; sometimes you must cross them out.

Adjective Clauses

Name_____ **Date** _____

Maze

Directions: Find your way from the start to the end by passing only through areas containing sentences that use commas correctly. If you're on the right path, you'll go through 7 correctly punctuated sentences. Be careful: There are false paths.

☀ **Bonus:** How many correctly punctuated sentences are there in the entire maze? _____

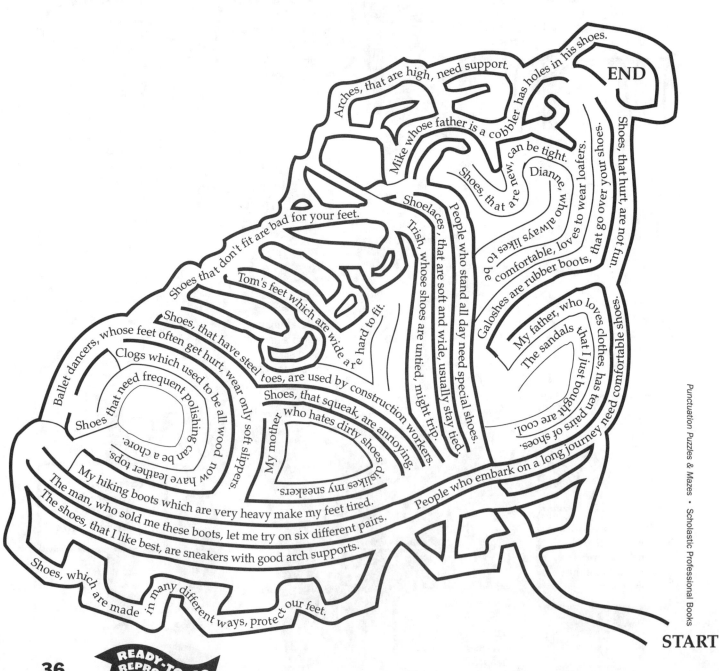

Arches, that are high, need support.

Mike whose father is a cobbler has holes in his shoes.

END

Shoes, that are new, can be tight.

Shoelaces, that are soft and wide, usually stay tied.

Shoes, that are new, can be tight.

Dianne who always likes to be comfortable, loves to wear loafers.

Shoes that go over your shoes.

Shoes, that hurt, are not fun.

Shoes that don't fit are bad for your feet.

Tom's feet which are wide are hard to fit.

Trish, whose shoes are untied, might trip.

People who stand all day need special shoes.

Galoshes are rubber boots, that go over your shoes.

My father, who loves clothes, has ten pairs of shoes.

The sandals that I just bought are cool.

Shoes, that have steel toes, are used by construction workers.

Ballet dancers, whose feet often get hurt, wear only soft slippers.

Clogs which used to be all wood now have leather tops.

Shoes that need frequent polishing can be a chore.

Shoes, that squeak, are annoying.

My mother who hates dirty shoes dislikes my sneakers.

My hiking boots which are very heavy make my feet tired.

People who embark on a long journey need comfortable shoes.

The man, who sold me these boots, let me try on six different pairs.

The shoes, that I like best, are sneakers with good arch supports.

Shoes, which are made in many different ways, protect our feet.

START

READY-TO-GO REPRODUCIBLES

Punctuation Puzzles & Mazes • Scholastic Professional Books

Unit 8: Adverb Clauses

If adverb clauses introduce or interrupt sentences, they are set off with commas.

Adverb clauses usually are not set off with commas when they end sentences.

This unit focuses on adverb clauses, which usually begin with a subordinating conjunction such as *if*, *although*, *as*, *when*, and *unless*. Adverb clauses often can be moved about in a sentence, changing the rhythm and the stress but not the factual meaning. The exercises in this unit help students identify and properly set off adverb clauses with commas.

Definition: A *subordinate clause* is a group of related words that has a subject and a verb and is part of a larger sentence. An *adverb clause* is a subordinate clause that modifies a verb, adjective, or adverb.

> **Rule:** An adverb clause is set off with commas when it introduces or interrupts a sentence. When it ends a sentence, it is usually not set off.

Examples:

After I read the lengthy directions, I decided to do the assignment at home.
  (introductory clause)

I decided, after I read the lengthy directions, to do the assignment at home.
  (interrupting clause)

I decided to do the assignment at home after I read the lengthy directions.
  (ending clause)

Mini-Lesson

Setting off adverb clauses with commas is easy to master as long as students can recognize the adverb clauses in the first place. To help your students recognize adverb clauses, ask them to come up with as many of those signal words, the subordinating conjunctions, as they can. Make

Adverb Clauses

the exercise enjoyable by writing sentences on the board that are missing conjunctions and have your students come up with words that will fill the slots. Make sure that several conjunctions will work in each space, and put the adverb clauses at both the beginning and ending of the sentences.

Examples:

_____ I don't understand, I'll ask my father.
(Possible subordinating conjunctions: *Because, Since, If*)

I memorized the poem _____ I walked to school.
(Possible subordinating conjunctions: *as, after, before, while, when*)

_____ I really want dessert, I'm not going to have any.
(Possible subordinating conjunctions: *Unless, Although, Even though, Though*)

Answers

Page 39, Hidden Message
1. When Flora first learned to swim, she wanted to go swimming as often as she could. **2.** Although Jessica prefers the backstroke, she can also swim freestyle. **3.** Before they learn how to swim, most people first learn how to float. **4.** Whenever it's a hot weekend, Flora's parents try take her to a swimming pool since she loves to swim so very much. **5.** Jessica's father, because he hurt his back, can swim but can't dive. **6.** Although she often wishes she could swim alone, Flora knows that she shouldn't go into the water unless another swimmer is with her. **7.** Jessica, even though she likes to swim, often would rather just lie on a towel by the pool and read while others play in the water. **8.** Flora is usually very tired at night if she has swum all day. **9.** Since she is Flora's best friend, Jessica swims more often than she would really like to. **10.** If, like Flora, you wish to become a competitive swimmer, then you must expect to train hard until you develop strong muscles. **Message:** NO

Page 40, Maze
The correct path goes through: 1. If you like to play baseball, then you usually like to play softball too. **2.** Even if you think it's a foul, try to catch it. **3.** If you are ready, we'll start the game. **4.** We put in a relief pitcher when our starter got tired. **5.** Even if you don't win, baseball is usually fun. **6.** If you bunt the ball, you must run fast to first. **7.** I've played since I was six years old. **8.** If a ball is hit long and high, it's very easy to misjudge it. **9.** If you drop a fly, base runners can run. **10.** You should try to relax before you bat.

READY·TO·GO REPRODUCIBLES

Name_____ **Date** _____

Hidden Message

Flora and Jessica are trying to decide if the water in the stream is deep enough to dive in. By correctly punctuating the sentences below, you can reveal the message and find out if it is safe to take that dive.

Directions: Make corrections, only when necessary, by inserting commas into the spaces. Then shade the stone in the bridge that matches the number of the space under each correction you've made. When you finish, a message will appear in the shaded stones. The first one has been done for you.

Hint: Be careful! Many of the spaces are in places where no commas should be inserted.

1. When Flora first learned to swim **,** she wanted to go swimming __ as often as she could.
   $\quad$ 25 $\qquad\qquad\qquad\qquad\qquad$ 1

2. Although Jessica prefers the backstroke__ she can also swim freestyle.
   $\qquad\qquad\qquad\qquad\qquad$ 13

3. Before they learn how to swim__ most people first learn how to float.
   $\qquad\qquad\qquad$ 6

4. Whenever it's a hot weekend__ Flora's parents try take her to a swimming pool__
   $\qquad\qquad\qquad\qquad$ 4 $\qquad\qquad\qquad\qquad\qquad\qquad\qquad\qquad$ 18

   since she loves to swim so very much.

5. Jessica's father__ because he hurt his back__ can swim but can't dive.
   $\qquad\qquad$ 29 $\qquad\qquad\qquad\qquad$ 11

6. Although she often wishes she could swim alone__ Flora knows that she shouldn't go
   $\qquad\qquad\qquad\qquad\qquad\qquad\qquad$ 3

   into the water__ unless another swimmer is with her.
   $\qquad\qquad$ 22

7. Jessica__ even though she likes to swim__ often would rather just
   $\qquad$ 26 $\qquad\qquad\qquad\qquad\qquad$ 5

   lie on a towel by the pool and read__ while others play in the water.
   $\qquad\qquad\qquad\qquad\qquad\qquad$ 20

8. Flora is usually very tired at night__ if she has swum all day.
   $\qquad\qquad\qquad\qquad\qquad\qquad$ 16

9. Since she is Flora's best friend__ Jessica swims more often__ than she would really like to.
   $\qquad\qquad\qquad\qquad$ 28 $\qquad\qquad\qquad\qquad\qquad$ 9

10. If, like Flora, you wish to become a competitive swimmer__ then
    $\qquad\qquad\qquad\qquad\qquad\qquad\qquad\qquad\qquad$ 14

    you must expect to train hard__ until you develop strong muscles.
    $\qquad\qquad\qquad\qquad$ 15

Name_____ **Date** _____

Maze

Directions: You can't snag a hot line drive with this glove, but you can work your way carefully from start to finish by passing through 10 areas with correctly punctuated sentences. Avoid sentences with misused or missing commas.

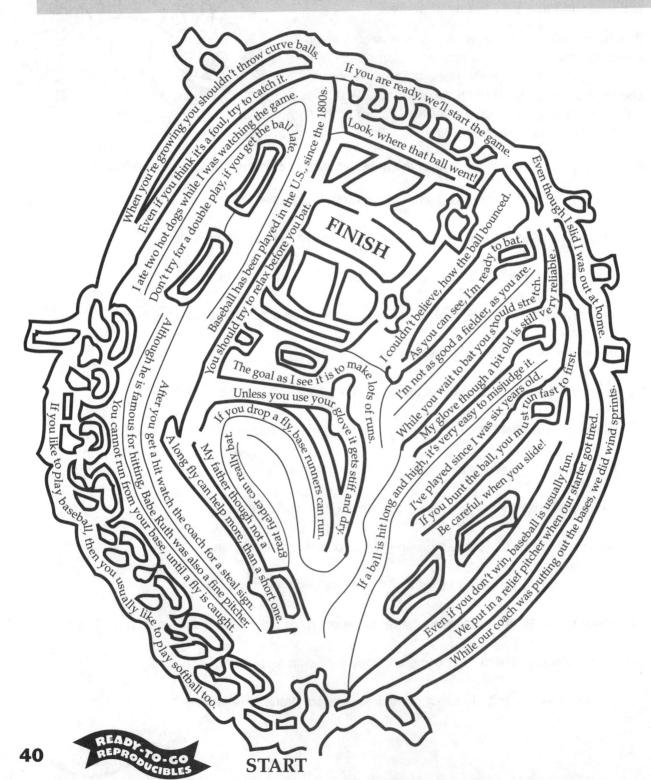

START

Unit 9: Direct Addresses, Unemphatic Exclamations, and Parenthetical Expressions

Yes, Robin, I do, as a matter of fact, know how to use commas.

This unit deals with punctuating three kinds of phrases that are somewhat related. These interrupting phrases have fancy names but are simple to recognize: *nominative of direct address* (henceforth called simply *direct address*), *unemphatic exclamations*, and *parenthetical expressions*.

Definition: A *direct address* occurs when one speaker addresses another directly by using a name or title. Only one comma is necessary to set off the name if the direct address begins or ends the sentence, but two commas should be used if the address interrupts the sentence.

Examples:

Marcia, you look ill.

Do you think, *Doctor*, that I'm getting the flu?

Definition: *Unemphatic exclamations*, which occur most often in dialogue, include comments like *yes*, *no*, *oh*, and *well*. These words are punctuated just like direct address, with one comma when they are the first (or, very rarely, the last) word in the sentence and with two commas when they interrupt it.

Examples:

"*Oh*, there you are," said Ariana.

"I think that, *yes*, I will have dessert," Hakim replied.

Well, dear reader, it is time for me to wrap this up.

As the last example illustrates, unemphatic exclamations are often used along with direct address, and sometimes two unemphatic exclamations are used in tandem. Usually commas are placed between these items even if there is no pause, but writers can use their own discretion and omit a comma if they wish to insist that there be no pause in the dialogue. Both of these examples are correct:

"*Oh, yes*, Veronica, I do love you!" sighed Roger.

"*Oh yes*, Veronica, I do love you!" sighed Roger.

Direct Addresses, Unemphatic Exclamations, and Parenthetical Expressions

Definition: *Parenthetical expressions* are common interrupting words and phrases that we use to connect ideas, provide transitions from one topic to the next, and aid conversation. Here are some of the most common ones:

however	indeed	after all	to tell the truth
therefore	nevertheless	on the other hand	on the contrary
first	naturally	I am sure	obviously
second	for example	I believe	as you can see
finally	of course	in my opinion	I hope

These expressions should be set off with commas. Again, we use only one comma when the parenthetical expression begins or ends a sentence and two when it interrupts the sentence. However, we only use commas to set off the expression if it is being used in a parenthetical way.

Examples:

Obviously, this sentence is an example of a parenthetical usage.

He was *obviously* upset. (not a parenthetical usage of *obviously*)

Mini-Lesson

After you teach these concepts, a good way to reinforce them is to have the students make up two kinds of sentences on their own. First, have them make up one sentence in which they use all three of the comma rules (take, for example, the one in the cartoon on page 41). Have them share their sentences, telling, as they read them aloud, where they used commas and why. Second, have them write pairs of sentences that use the same word or expression, one in which the word or expression needs to be set off and one in which it does not.

Examples:

The *doctor* is in.

I've found *no* problem.

Finally, I'm done.

Now, *Doctor*, please don't hurt me.

No, there isn't a problem.

I'm *finally* done.

Answers

Page 43, Riddle
Correctly punctuated sentences: **1.** Yes, Marci, your new haircut really suits you. **2.** Jeff thinks, on the contrary, that Marci's haircut is too short. **3.** Oh, Jeff, aren't you being too critical? **4.** It's strange, isn't it, how haircuts seem so important to us. **5.** Didn't you know, Carla, that hair and fur are different? **6.** Marci, of course, knows that animals with fur shed. **7.** Well, Marci, did you know that poodles have hair rather than fur? **8.** Jeff, however, wishes that he had fur so he'd never need another haircut. **9.** Haircuts, in my opinion, are nothing to get upset about. **10.** No, Marci, your haircut really looks great! **11.** Don't be a comic, Carlos, and ask Marci why she's wearing a hat.
Answer to riddle: It is a coffin.

Page 44, Maze
The correct path passes through: 1. Well, you should know, Mr. Tan, that there are 30,000 species of spider. **2.** Some spiders, it seems, live twenty years. **3.** Yes, sir, I like most spiders. **4.** This, Roy, is not a nice spot. **5.** No, spiders can't be related to scorpions! **6.** Spider webs are, in fact, extremely strong. **7.** Fran, on the contrary, loves all bugs. **8.** Of course, Mara, I know that spiders eat many pests. **9.** This spider, on the other hand, may be dangerous. **10.** That, my friend, is truly not a black widow. **11.** Spiders, I think you all know, are arachnids. **12.** Well, I'm not lost!

Page 45, Word Find
1. Electricity, in my opinion, is … **2.** Can you imagine a world, my dear reader, without … **3.** Television, for instance, couldn't … **4.** Yes, we … flashlights and fans, for example. **5.** Our ancestors, to be sure, lived … **6.** Well, sir, they … **7.** I wonder, my friend, if … **8.** Many people, however, find …

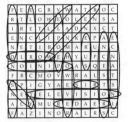

Punctuation Puzzles & Mazes • Scholastic Professional Books

Name_____ Date _____

Riddle

The man who makes it doesn't want it.
The man who buys it doesn't need it.
The man who uses it doesn't know it.
What is it?

Answer

___ ___ ___i ___ ___ ___ ___ ___ ___ ___ ___ .
 6   4   1   2   5   11 10 3   8   7   9

Directions: To check your answer to this riddle, complete the exercise below. In each example insert a comma to correctly punctuate the sentence. Then underline the letter that comes right before the comma you inserted. Write that letter in the answer space with the number that matches the number of the sentence. The first one has been done for you.

1. Yes, Marci, your new haircut really suits you.

2. Jeff thinks on the contrary, that Marci's haircut is too short.

3. Oh, Jeff aren't you being too critical?

4. It's strange, isn't it how haircuts seem so important to us.

5. Didn't you know, Carla that hair and fur are different?

6. Marci of course, knows that animals with fur shed.

7. Well, Marci did you know that poodles have hair rather than fur?

8. Jeff however, wishes that he had fur so he'd never need another haircut.

9. Haircuts, in my opinion are nothing to get upset about.

10. No Marci, your haircut really looks great!

11. Don't be a comic Carlos, and ask Marci why she's wearing a hat.

Direct Addresses, Unemphatic Exclamations, and Parenthetical Expressions

Name_____   Date_____

Maze

Directions: Work your way through this spider maze by tracing a path through 12 areas that contain sentences in which commas are used correctly. Avoid areas that contain missing or misused commas for direct addresses, parenthetical expressions, and unemphatic exclamations like *yes* and *well*.

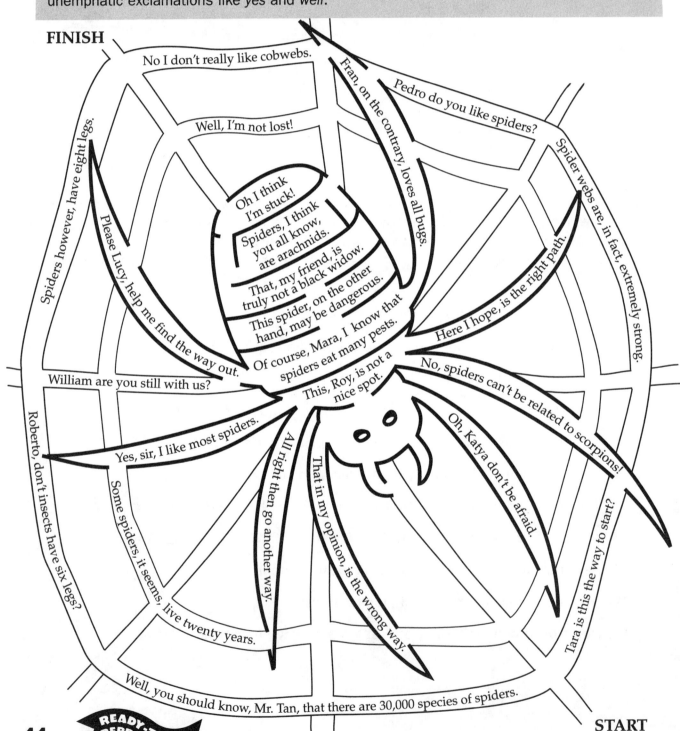

FINISH

No I don't really like cobwebs.

Fran, on the contrary, loves all bugs.

Pedro do you like spiders?

Spider webs are, in fact, extremely strong.

Well, I'm not lost!

Spiders however, have eight legs.

Oh I think I'm stuck!

Spiders, I think you all know, are arachnids.

That, my friend, is truly not a black widow.

This spider, on the other hand, may be dangerous.

Of course, Mara, I know that spiders eat many pests.

Here I hope, is the right path.

Please Lucy, help me find the way out.

William are you still with us?

This, Roy, is not a nice spot.

No, spiders can't be related to scorpions!

Roberto, don't insects have six legs?

Yes, sir, I like most spiders.

Some spiders, it seems, live twenty years.

All right then go another way.

That in my opinion, is the wrong way.

Oh, Katya don't be afraid.

Tara is this the way to start?

Well, you should know, Mr. Tan, that there are 30,000 species of spiders.

START

READY-TO-GO REPRODUCIBLES

Name_____ Date _____

Word Find

Directions: Solve the word find by locating words found in the sentences below. Correct those sentences that are missing commas. When you insert a comma, underline the word right before the comma. Find each of the words that you underlined in the word-find grid.

Hints: Since there are 16 commas missing, there will be 16 words for you to find. The words in the word find run up and down, left and right, and diagonally.

1. Electricity in my opinion is usually taken for granted.

2. Can you imagine a world my dear reader without electricity?

3. Television for instance couldn't exist.

4. Yes we would be without many comforting things—like flashlights and fans for example.

5. Our ancestors to be sure lived very well without the electrical appliances that we call vital.

6. Well sir they were probably not as safe or comfortable as we are.

7. I wonder my friend if you could live a whole week without any electric power.

8. Many people however find that it can be fun to have the power fail for a short time.

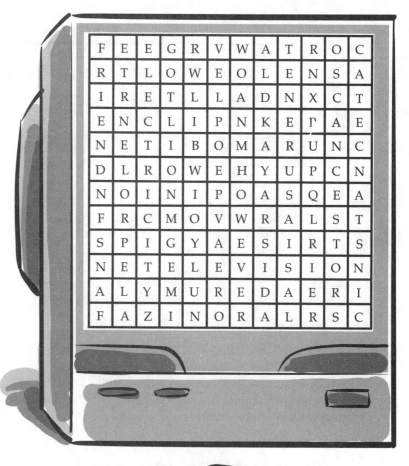

F	E	E	G	R	V	W	A	T	R	O	C
R	T	L	O	W	E	O	L	E	N	S	A
I	R	E	T	L	L	A	D	N	X	C	T
E	N	C	L	I	P	N	K	E	Γ	A	E
N	E	T	I	B	O	M	A	R	U	N	C
D	L	R	O	W	E	H	Y	U	P	C	N
N	O	I	N	I	P	O	A	S	Q	E	A
F	R	C	M	O	V	W	R	A	L	S	T
S	P	I	G	Y	A	E	S	I	R	T	S
N	E	T	E	L	E	V	I	S	I	O	N
A	L	Y	M	U	R	E	D	A	E	R	I
F	A	Z	I	N	O	R	A	L	R	S	C

Unit 10: Quotations at the Beginning of a Sentence

"**Where does the question mark go in a quotation __**" asked Robin.

"**At the end of the quotation, not the end of the sentence,**" said Jay.

Because quotations cause such frequent punctuation and capitalization problems, there are three separate units devoted to them. In this unit the quotation always comes first; in Unit 11 it always comes last. In Unit 12 both of these types are reviewed and the added difficulty of divided quotations is combined with the first two types.

Rule 1: When a quotation comes first, preceding the explanatory *he said* or *she asked*, the first letter of the word following the quoted material remains lowercase.

Example:

"Where is my pen?" she asked. (not "Where is my pen?" *She* asked.)

Rule 2: In sentences in which the quotation comes first, the endmark of the quoted material is placed inside the closing quotation mark. When the quoted material is a statement and would require a period, use a comma.

Example:

"I've found your pen," he declared. (not "I've found your pen." he declared.)

Teaching Tips

★ Students often make the mistake shown in the first example and capitalize the first word of the sentence outside the quoted words. This is a reasonable error; we would indeed need double capitalization if the sentence were rephrased *She asked, "Where is my pen?"*

Punctuation Puzzles & Mazes • Scholastic Professional Books

★ The most frequent punctuation problem for this kind of quotation is the misplacement of question marks and exclamation points. Sometimes these marks are incorrectly placed at the end of the sentence rather than inside the quotation marks at the end of the quotation: *"Where is my pen," she asked?* instead of *"Where is my pen?" she asked.*

★ Other common errors that the exercises in this unit address are punctuation placed outside the final quotation marks (*"Where is my pen"? she asked*) and double punctuation (*"Where is my pen?", she asked.*).

Mini-Lesson

By reviewing quotations in a step-by-step process, you can help students avoid the two usual problems in writing dialogue: (1) when to capitalize and (2) where to place punctuation marks.

A good way to begin is to stress the two parts of a quotation: *the writer's or narrator's part* in which the speaker of the quotation and the situation is described—*Throwing open the door, Alicia said happily to her mother*—and the speaker's part—*"Oh, you're home!"* This may seem elementary, but in the heat of composing, many young students, and even many adults, have trouble separating themselves from their characters. Thus the writer's and speaker's parts don't clearly stand out with their own—quite logical—punctuation and capitalization needs.

On the board, write memorable quotations that students contribute. Encourage them first to identify the writer's or narrator's part and the speaker's part and then to suggest appropriate punctuation. Figuring out punctuation for quotations is made easier if we think about just where the writer's part and the speaker's part separate.

Answers

Page 48, Hidden Message
1. "In the old days we used to have so much snow," said Samantha's grandfather. **2.** "We had six inches of snow last week," Samantha sighed, having heard many stories about the supposed good old days before. **3.** "Six inches is nothing!" exclaimed her grandfather. **4.** "Have you ever seen six feet of snow?" he continued. **5.** "No, not all at once," replied Samantha with another sigh. **6.** "Why, one winter the snow was so deep we had to come and go by the upstairs windows," her grandfather said proudly. **7.** "Wasn't it awfully dark and dreary downstairs?" asked Samantha. **8.** "Well, yes, but the worst was when my grandfather told me not to complain because when he was a kid the snow was over the roof!" laughed Samantha's grandfather with a big wink. **Word in flagstones:** ICY

Page 49, Maze
The correct path goes through: 1. "Could I ride on the elephant?" asked Maude. **2.** "This elephant is not full grown but already weighs three tons," said Sarah. **3.** "Such a small tail on this huge animal!" cried Maria. **4.** "I like zoos," stated Mia. **5.** "Is this a leg or a tree?" asked Paco. **6.** "He is so clever with his trunk," said Kile. **7.** "Indian elephants have smaller ears than African elephants," stated Lee. **8.** "Was he born here?" asked Erin. **9.** "I think I'll give him some peanuts," Lucia said. **10.** "His skin is baggy!" cried Sean. **11.** "Is he smiling?" asked Min. **12.** "Elephants are smart," said the guide. **13.** "Time to go," Darcy said. **14.** "Thanks!" exclaimed Tess.

Page 50, Coded Message
1. "What is your favorite invention?" asked Alicia. **2.** "Summer vacation!" shouted her brother Greg. **3.** "You're never serious," sighed Alicia. **4.** "Okay, give me a minute to think," said Greg. **5.** "Are you thinking up another joke?" asked Alicia. **6.** "No, I've got a good one!" said Greg with some excitement. **7.** "My favorite invention is simple but brings great joy," added Greg. **8.** "What can you be thinking of?" wondered Alicia. **9.** "Candy!" exclaimed Greg. **10.** "Why were brothers ever invented?" asked Alicia as she left the room. **Answer:** Thomas Alva Edison

1	2	3	4	5	6	7	8	9	10	11	12
A	T	E	R	H	O	T	M	U	A	L	S

13	14	15	16	17	18	19	20	21	22	23	24
V	I	A	R	Q	L	E	N	V	O	A	C

25	26	27	28	29	30	31	32	33	34	35	36
E	M	T	O	R	I	S	U	B	O	R	N

Name_____ **Date** _____

Hidden Message

Samantha is about to help her grandfather down the walk on a cold night in February. But if she could see the warning hidden in the flagstones, she might think twice about it. To discover the message, check the punctuation and capitalization of the following sentences.

Directions: Check for mistakes wherever you spot underlined letters and punctuation marks. For each underlined mistake, shade in the flagstone with the matching number in the drawing. The first one has been done for you.

Hint: Some of the underlined items are correct as they are,

1. "In the old days we used to have so much snow." said Samantha's grandfather.
6 21 40 22

2. "We had six inches of snow last week", Samantha sighed, having heard many stories
18 7

about the supposed good old days before.
1

3. "Six inches is nothing." exclaimed her grandfather!
55 35 11 12

4. "Have you ever seen six feet of snow?" He continued.
38 4 29 25

5. No, not all at once", Replied Samantha with another sigh.
42 9 24 50

6. "Why, one winter the snow was so deep we had to come and go by the upstairs
47

windows ", her grandfather said proudly.
14 2 20

7. "Wasn't it awfully dark and dreary downstairs," Asked Samantha?
16 41 22 44

8. "Well, yes, but the worst was when my grandfather told me not to complain because when
30

he was a kid the snow was over the roof." Laughed Samantha's grandfather witha big wink.
27 10 33

READY-TO-GO
REPRODUCIBLES

Punctuation Puzzles & Mazes • Scholastic Professional Books

Name_____ **Date** _____

Maze

Directions: Trace a path to the end through 14 sentences without mistakes in the capitalization and punctuation of quotations.

"This elephant is not full grown but already weighs three tons," said Sarah.

"Indian elephants have smaller ears than African elephants," stated Lee.

"He has such a kind face!" Exclaimed Mohammed.

"All elephants are vegetarians", said Brooke.

"Will he grow tusks?" Asked Kwami.

"He's coming over here," cried Roxanne!

"I wonder where he sleeps," Said Tai.

"Where is his mother? Asked Fran.

"Time to go," Darcy said.

"Could I ride on the elephant?" asked Maude.

"Elephants are fun," Said Tim.

"Was he born here?" asked Erin.

"Such a small tail on this huge animal!" cried Maria.

"He is so clever with his trunk," said Kile.

"He's trumpeting!" yelled Margo.

"He's huge!" Yelled Lin.

"I think I'll give him some peanuts," Lucia said.

"His skin is baggy!" cried Sean.

"Is he smiling?" asked Min.

"Elephants are smart," said the guide.

"Thanks!" exclaimed Tess.

"How old is he," asked Ari?

"Is this a leg or a tree?" asked Paco.

"I like zoos," stated Mia.

START

END

Quotations at the Beginning of a Sentence

Coded Message

Name _____   Date _____

"Genius is one percent inspiration and ninety-nine percent perspiration."

Do you know who said that?   Answer: _____ _____ _____

Directions: Who made the statement above? To find out, correct all the mistakes in punctuation and capitalization in the quotation sentences below. Go to the grid and circle the letter that matches the number under each mistake. The circled letters from the grid will spell out the answer. The first mistake has been corrected for you.

1. "What is your favorite invention?" *a* Asked Alicia.
   16 18   3

2. "Summer vacation," shouted her brother Greg!
   10 32   31

3. "You're never serious", Sighed Alicia.
   6   28   4

4. "Okay, give me a minute to think," Said Greg.
   1   5   13

5. "Are you thinking up another joke," asked Alicia?
   23 4   8

6. "No, I've got a good one," said Greg with some excitement!
   34 1   21

7. "My favorite invention is simple but brings great joy," Added Greg.
   11 12   26

8. "What can you be thinking of," wondered Alicia?
   30 1   36

9. "Candy!" Exclaimed Greg.
   26 15   33

10. "Why were brothers ever invented," asked Alicia as she left the room?
    2   20   25

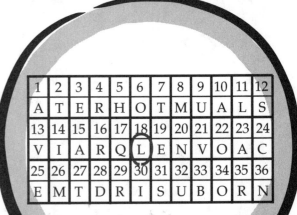

1	2	3	4	5	6	7	8	9	10	11	12
A	T	E	R	H	O	T	M	U	A	L	S
13	14	15	16	17	18	19	20	21	22	23	24
V	I	A	R	Q	L	E	N	V	O	A	C
25	26	27	28	29	30	31	32	33	34	35	36
E	M	T	D	R	I	S	U	B	O	R	N

Punctuation Puzzles & Mazes • Scholastic Professional Books

READY-TO-GO REPRODUCIBLES

Unit 11: Quotations at the End of a Sentence

> Robin asked, "**w** hy is there extra capitalization in this sentence?"

> Jay said, "**B** ecause the first quoted word begins the speaker's sentence."

This unit focuses on the punctuation and capitalization of quotations that are placed at the end of a sentence, after the writer's introductory words.

Rule 1: When a quotation comes last, following the explanatory *He said* or *She asked*, the first letter of the quotation is capitalized.

> **Example:**
>
> She asked, "*Who's there?*" (not She asked, "*who's there?*")

Rule 2: In sentences in which the quotation comes last, use a comma to set off the introductory material from the quotation.

Teaching Tips

⭐ In this arrangement students often forget to begin the quoted material with a capital letter. If students can think of this kind of quotation as really two sentences in one—the writer's and the speaker's—then the double capitalization will become reasonable. In the example above, *She* is capitalized because it is the first word of the author's sentence, and *Who's* is capitalized because it is the first word of the speaker's question.

⭐ The two most frequent punctuation problems for this kind of quotation are the omission of the comma after the writer's part (*She asked "Who's there?"*) and the misplacement of the end punctuation outside the final quotation marks (*She asked, "Who's there"?*). Occasionally, students see that there are two sentences in one and use double end punctuation (*She asked, "Who's there?". *). This is a very logical but nevertheless nonstandard practice.

Quotations at the End of a Sentence

Mini-Lesson

Since the key to the correct capitalization and punctuation of this kind of quotation lies in students' seeing that there are really two sentences in one in a quotation, it is a good idea to emphasize that the writer's portion of a quotation can be very short and the speaker's part can be very long (*Lincoln said, "Four score and seven years . . ."*).

It's also helpful to show students that the writer's portion can be a lengthy exposition followed by a very short speech (*After the masked ball, Maria, still dressed in her outlandish kangaroo costume, bounced out to the street where Rudyard was cowering and whispered ecstatically, "I'm so hoppy!"*). Dialogue can, obviously, be made up of any combination of narration and speech lengths, but in each dialogue sentence, one part is an introductory or expanded sentence by the writer and the other part is the quoted material.

To firmly establish this idea of a two-part dialogue sentence, pass out a sheet with a half dozen unpunctuated quotations. Make sure that some of the quotations have long writer's introductions and some have long speeches, and be sure to include questions and exclamations as well as statements. Ask each student to underline only the writers' introductions, not the speakers' words. Then have the students exchange papers and correctly punctuate the quotations that follow the underlined parts, remembering also to capitalize the first word of each quotation.

Answers

Page 53, Maze
The correct path to the finish goes through:
1. Mr. Washington said, "Welcome to Lake LaBelle Summer Camp." **2.** Maria asked, "Is there enough gas to mow the fields?" **3.** Coach Hannah explained, "In other countries soccer is usually called football, and they rarely play the game we Americans call football." **4.** Tony called out, "Ice cream with fresh strawberries for anyone who's still hungry!" **5.** Aaron asked, "Is the wind strong enough for sailing?" **6.** Carl said, "Don't forget the sunblock." **7.** The director asked, "Is it going to rain?" **8.** Brandy sighed, "Those kids are fun but tiring!" **9.** Doug whispered, "Are you asleep?" **10.** Tanya called out, "Sweet dreams!"

Page 54, Question and Answer
Corrections: 1. Martina exclaimed, "I love the Fourth of July!" **2.** Martina's mother asked, "What is it that you like so much about that holiday?" **3.** Martina said, "The fireworks displays are what I like best." **4.** Her mother agreed, "The pyrotechnics can be spectacular." **5.** Martina asked, "Are pyrotechnics the same as fireworks?" **6.** Her mother explained, "Pyrotechnics comes from Greek and literally means fire arts." **7.** Martina cried, "I'd love to be a fire artist!" **8.** Her mother laughed and said, "One day you could be if you wanted, but please don't start practicing without telling me."
Answer: John Philip Sousa

Page 55–56, Story
There were errors in the following sentences (corrections underlined) **1.** Wanda tapped William on the shoulder and said with a smirk, "Roses are red, and often they're pink; there's a present for you—just go look in the sink." **2.** After thinking a bit, William . . . replied, "Roses are pink but usually red. You can find your own present out in the shed." **3.** Continuing . . . William smiled and asked, "Since I like the sunshine and you like the shade, then would you consider making a trade?" **4.** Wanda happily exclaimed, "Roses are red—go right ahead!" **5.** Wanda exclaimed incredulously, "I think I'd rather eat my hat than go along with a deal like that!" **6.** He said, "I just don't know what could be wrong since cutting the grass takes you so long." **7.** She asked William, "If I do all those extra dishes, will you then grant me one of my wishes?" **8.** With a look . . . Wanda intoned, "I wish upon a lovely star . . . that you will help me wash the car." **9.** William cried, "It's very, very plain to see that you're just out to swindle me!" **10.** She . . . called, "Kids, where are you?" **11.** William called back, "Upstairs, Mom!" **12.** Their mother . . . said, "If you don't get going, I'm going to make my request less poetic." **13.** Wanda . . . called, "Okay, Mom, I'm on the run, and in just one hour the grass will be done." **14.** William . . . said, "The dishes will be done well too, and we might just wash the car for you."

READY-TO-GO REPRODUCIBLES

Maze

Name_____ **Date**_____

Directions: Trace a path to the finish following 10 correctly written quotations. Avoid ones with mistakes.

Hint: You may also follow the dotted lines across the lake if the areas on both sides contain correctly written quotations.

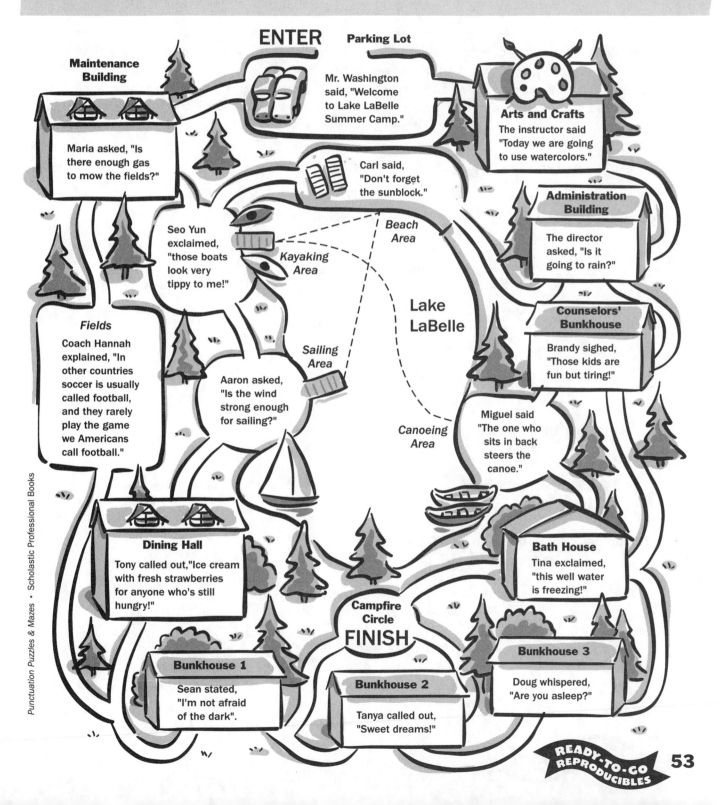

ENTER

Parking Lot

Maintenance Building

Maria asked, "Is there enough gas to mow the fields?"

Mr. Washington said, "Welcome to Lake LaBelle Summer Camp."

Arts and Crafts
The instructor said "Today we are going to use watercolors."

Carl said, "Don't forget the sunblock."

Administration Building
The director asked, "Is it going to rain?"

Seo Yun exclaimed, "those boats look very tippy to me!"

Beach Area

Kayaking Area

Lake LaBelle

Counselors' Bunkhouse
Brandy sighed, "Those kids are fun but tiring!"

Fields
Coach Hannah explained, "In other countries soccer is usually called football, and they rarely play the game we Americans call football."

Sailing Area

Aaron asked, "Is the wind strong enough for sailing?"

Canoeing Area

Miguel said "The one who sits in back steers the canoe."

Dining Hall
Tony called out,"Ice cream with fresh strawberries for anyone who's still hungry!"

Bath House
Tina exclaimed, "this well water is freezing!"

Campfire Circle
FINISH

Bunkhouse 1
Sean stated, "I'm not afraid of the dark".

Bunkhouse 2
Tanya called out, "Sweet dreams!"

Bunkhouse 3
Doug whispered, "Are you asleep?"

Name_____ Date _____

Question and Answer

Question: What man who was in the U. S. Marine Corps became known as "The March King"?

Answer: __ __ __ __ __ __ i __ __ __ __ __ __ __ __
       1   2   3   4   5   6   7   8   9 10 11 12 13 14 15

Directions: Discover the answer as you correct punctuation and capitalization mistakes in the quotations below. Circle the number and letter under each mistake you've corrected. Then find the answer space with the matching number and write the letter in that space. The first one has been done for you.

1. Martina exclaimed , "I love the Fourth of July!"
                 (7-I) 2-A   14-N

2. Martina's mother asked, "what is it that you like so much about that holiday"?
                  6-K 15-A   2-O

3. Martina said "the fireworks displays are what I like best."
           5-P 12-O   9-R

4. Her mother agreed, "The pyrotechnics can be spectacular".
               1-B 13-L   9-I

5. Martina asked "are pyrotechnics the same as fireworks"?
           3-H 14-S   8-L

6. Her mother said, "*pyrotechnics* comes from the Greek
            3-L 1-J

    and literally means *fire arts*".
                  13-U

7. Martina cried "I'd love to be a fire artist!"
           4-N 9-W   15-E

8. Her mother laughed and said "one day you could be if you
                 6-H 10-P

    wanted, but please don't start practicing without telling me".
                                      11-S

Punctuation Puzzles & Mazes • Scholastic Professional Books

Story

Name_____ Date _____

Directions: The story below is full of dialogue and full of errors in punctuation and capitalization! Find all 23 mistakes and correct them. Use the underlined areas to help you through the first part of the story. (Be careful! Not all the underlined areas contain errors.) Then, find the mistakes on your own in the second half of the story.

Wanda and William were twins and very fond of each other, but they were also mischievous and competitive. Sometimes they liked to tease each other or to see who could get the best of a situation. This was one of those times.

Wanda tapped William on the shoulder and said with a smirk, "roses are red, and often they're pink; there's a present for you—just go look in the sink."

After thinking a bit, William, who knew exactly what his sister was talking about, replied "Roses are pink but usually red. You can find your own present out in the shed".

You've probably already guessed that they were kidding one another about chores that they each had to do. It was William's turn to do the dishes and Wanda's turn to take out the lawn mower and cut the grass.

Continuing the rhyming game that Wanda had started, William smiled and asked, "Since I like the sunshine and you like shade, then would you consider making a trade"?

Wanda happily exclaimed, "roses are red—go right ahead."!

After more thought William proceeded, "If you do the dishes for me five times, I'll mow the grass without more rhymes."

Wanda exclaimed incredulously "I think I'd rather eat my hat than go along with a deal like that"!

William couldn't help himself and started laughing. He said "I just don't know what could be wrong since cutting the grass takes you so long".

Wanda had an idea of her own. She asked William, "if I do all those extra dishes, will you then grant one of my wishes?"

William laughed and said, "If you first tell me what that wish is, I just might change my deal for the dishes."

(Keep up the good work! There are 12 more corrections to make, but there is no more underlining to help you.)

Name_____   **Date** _____

Story (part 2)

With a look of mock seriousness, Wanda intoned "I wish upon a lovely star—and a star, my William, is what you are—that you will help me wash the car".

William cried, "it's very, very plain to see that you're just out to swindle me!"

Wanda did not like that accusation at all and was about to make an angry reply—with the rhymes forgotten—when suddenly they heard their mother calling from the bottom of the stairs.

She sounded a bit impatient when she called "kids, where are you"?

William called back, "upstairs, Mom!"

Thinking that she would take a witty approach rather than a critical one, their mother decided to make up a little poem and said, "While the roses are redding and the violets are bluing, there are some chores that you both should be doing."

William and Wanda couldn't answer because they both were laughing too hard.

Their mother tried again and said "if you don't get going, I'm going to make my request less poetic."

Wanda winked at William and called, "Okay, Mom, I'm on the run, and in just one hour the grass will be done".

William took her lead and said "the dishes will be done well too, and we might just wash the car for you."

Punctuation Puzzles & Mazes • Scholastic Professional Books

READY·TO·GO REPRODUCIBLES

Unit 12: Divided Quotations

"How do I know**,**" asked Robin**,** "what punctuation to use when a quotation is interrupted?"

"You must see if both parts of your quotation are complete thoughts**,**" Jay replied**.** "If so, you must use a period or semicolon between the parts."

The exercises that follow review the concepts of the last two units—sentences in which the quotations come first and sentences in which they come last. In addition, the tricky problem of divided quotations is covered in these often challenging exercises.

Rule: In sentences with *divided quotations*, punctuation and capitalization depend on whether the opening words of a speaker form a complete sentence or whether they are connected to the second half of the quotation.

Example:

The following examples illustrate the major difficulties of divided quotations, with the typical trouble spots in boldface:

"If you're ever in town**,**" she said**,** "**l**et's get together."

"I am in town**,**" he said**.** "**L**et's get together."

Notice that in the first example the first part of the quotation is not a complete thought; there is thus a comma after *she said* and a lowercase *l* for *let's*, the first word of the continued quotation. In the second example both parts of the quotation are complete thoughts, thus the need for the period after *he said* and the capital *L* for *Let's*.

Mini-Lesson

After a quick review of the simpler forms of quotations—ones where the writer's part comes first or last—you can address the stickier problem of divided quotations. It's almost impossible for students to punctuate these complex quotations properly without a good understanding of run-on sentences (*Give me that candy it's mine*) and sentence fragments (*If you don't give me that candy*). (See Units 3, 4, and 5 for more on sentence fragments and run-ons.)

Divided Quotations

Write the above run-on example, or one like it, on the board and ask someone in the class how to punctuate it properly. You'll probably get this suggestion: *Give me that candy! It's mine!* Or perhaps: *Give me that candy. It's mine.*

Now ask someone to insert correctly the words *the little boy said* between those sentences. (If this is a preliminary lesson rather than review, first warn the class that the writer's part should be punctuated as it normally would be if it were following only the first of the two sentences.) Lead the class to the following result: *"Give me that candy," the little boy said. "It's mine."*

Now add this sentence beneath the correctly punctuated quotation: *You should give me that candy because it's mine.* After establishing that this is only one complete thought, ask a student to insert the same writer's words—*the little boy said*—into the quotation without turning one of the parts of the original sentence into a fragment. If the student ends up with the incorrect form (*"You should give me that candy," the little boy said. "Because it's mine."*), have other students help out. They should be able to suggest substituting a comma for the first period and a lowercase *b* in the second part of the quotation to keep the original sentence together.

Repeat this exercise a few times with other divided quotations, some of them needing only a comma after the writer's part and some of them needing a period. Stress that students must look at both parts of the quotation to determine whether they are complete thoughts or form a single sentence.

Answers

Page 59, Question and Answer
1. Carver...Mike, "Who...to?" **2.** "Now...of?" said...Carver. **3.** "Well," said Carver, "from...on." **4.** "Now...sweet!" exclaimed...horror. **5.** Carver retorted, "And...annoying!" **6.** "Okay," said...proudly, "I'll...peanuts." **7.** Carver said, "Hundreds...cost." **8.** Mike...replied, "Products...them." **9.** "At...made," laughed Carver, "a...believe." **10.** "Do...potatoes?" asked Mike. **11.** "Yes...remember," said...Carver, "that...bicycle!" **12.** "Well...George Washington," Mike continued, "I'm...bicycle."
Question: Who made hundreds of products from peanuts and sweet potatoes?
Answer: George Washington Carver

Page 60, Grid Message
Corrected sentences: 1. "I wonder," said Paula, "where Katmandu is." **2.** "Katmandu is the capital of Nepal and is near Mount Everest," replied her father. **3.** Paula's mother asked her, "Why are you interested in Katmandu?" **4.** "Because," answered Paula, "the word is so strange and lovely." **5.** "It also makes me imagine a cat man!" she exclaimed. **6.** Her father laughed, "That's wonderful, even if you are pronouncing Katmandu incorrectly, like *catman* instead of *cahtmahn*." **7.** "Either way it's nice," said Paula, "and I'd love to go there." **8.** "Do you know how hard it is to get to Nepal?" asked her mother. **9.** Paula replied, "Well, I know that Nepal is in Asia, and that's far away." **10.** "I think that if you really want to go," said her mother, "then one day you probably will—and maybe you'll even see a cat man."
Message: You are a good editor.

Page 61, Maze
The correct path goes through: 1. "Swans are such regal birds!" exclaimed Mia.
2. Brenda asked, "Are all swans mute?"
3. "Look!" cried Rosalinda. **4.** Ari asked, "What's its name?" **5.** "When's lunch?" asked Pia. **6.** "Sometimes," said Ted, "swans can drive away ducks and geese." **7.** "I think," said Katya, "that the swan is tired."
8. Brenda cried, "The swan just bit my finger!"
9. "Yummy!" exclaimed Pia.
Bonus: 18 **Also: 1.** "I think," said Sula, "that ducks are nice too." **2.** "Is it true that swans mate for life?" asked Annelise. **3.** Lucia exclaimed, "It's a beautiful bird on a beautiful day!" **4.** "There are swans in fairy tales," said Nan. **5.** Min cried, "Wow!" **6.** Pia said, "I'm hungry." **7.** "Is she okay?" asked Di.
8. "Hey," shouted Pia, "I'm really starved!"
9. "Jane said, "It's time to go."

Question and Answer

Name_____ Date _____

Directions: To discover both a coded question and its answer, correct the punctuation and capitalization in the sentences below. When you make a correction, write the underlined word from the section you've corrected in the matching space above. The first example has been done for you.

Question: <u>Who</u> _____ _____ _____ _____
             1   2   3   4   5

_____ _____ _____ _____ _____?
   6   7   8   9   10

Answer: _____ _____
           11   12

1. Carver asked his friend <u>Mike</u>, "<u>who</u> does that fantastic bicycle belong <u>to</u>?"
                    9   1   3

2. "Now what bike might you be thinking <u>of</u>"? <u>said</u> Mike with a wink at <u>Carver</u>.
   6   4   2   8

3. "<u>Well</u>," <u>said</u> Carver, "<u>From</u> where I'm <u>standing</u>, there seems to be
   2   5   11   6

only one bike in sight—the one you're sitting <u>on</u>."
                                         3

4. "<u>Now</u> that sarcastic tone was not at all <u>sweet</u>"! <u>exclaimed</u> Mike in mock <u>horror</u>.
   10   9   12   7

5. Carver <u>retorted</u>, "<u>and</u> your games aren't sweet either—just <u>annoying</u>!"
         9   8   4

6. "<u>Okay</u>," said Mike proudly, "<u>I'll</u> inform you that the bike is mine, and, believe me, it didn't cost
   10   2   6

just <u>peanuts</u>".
    7

7. Carver <u>said</u>, "<u>hundreds</u> of dollars is what I'd say it <u>cost</u>."
     11   3   5

8. Mike nodded and <u>replied</u>, "<u>products</u> like this beauty cost so much that my family can't really
                8   5

afford <u>them</u>."
    10

9. "At last you've <u>made</u>", <u>laughed</u> Carver, "a statement that I can <u>believe</u>."
   3   2   7   12

10. "<u>Do</u> you know that super store that sells everything from hardware to <u>potatoes</u>"? asked <u>Mike</u>.
   6   10   4

11. "Yes, and now I <u>remember</u>," <u>said</u> a suddenly wide-<u>eyed</u> Carver. "that they had a raffle for a new <u>bicycle</u>!"
   3   11   9   12   2   8

12. "Well, like <u>George Washington</u>", <u>Mike</u> <u>continued</u>, "<u>I'm</u> not telling a
   5   11   6   12   4

lie when I say that I won that raffle and this is my <u>bicycle</u>."
                                              3

Quotations

Divided Quotations

Grid Message

Directions: Correct all capitalization and punctuation mistakes in the quotation examples below. For each mistake write the letter that follows the coordinate in the appropriate grid square. When you have finished, the grid will reveal a message. The first one has been done for you.

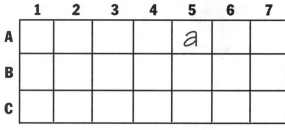

	1	2	3	4	5	6	7
A					a		
B							
C							

1. "I wonder," Said Paula, "where Katmandu is".
   C2-R   A5-A   B4-S   C2-D

2. "Katmandu is the capital of Nepal and is near Mount Everest",
   C6-M   B3-G

   replied her father.
   A7-T   C7-N

3. Paula's mother asked her, "why are you interested in Katmandu?"
                              A2-O   C3-P

4. "Because," Answered Paula, "The word is so strange and lovely."
   B2-T   A7-E   B1-A   C2-W

5. "It also makes me imagine a cat man", she exclaimed!
   B7-C   C6-R   B5-O

6. Her father laughed, "that's wonderful, even if you are
                       A1-Y

   pronouncing Katmandu incorrectly, like *catman* instead of *cahtmahn*".
                                                              C3-I

7. "Either way it's nice," Said Paula, "and I'd love to go there".
   A6-U   C5-O   A4-W   B4-O

8. "Do you know how hard it is to get to Nepal," asked her mother?
   B2-L   A3-U   B6-D

9. Paula replied, "well, I know that Nepal is in Asia, and that's far away."
              A6-R   C7-S

10. "I think that if you really want to go," Said her mother, "Then
    B2-Y   C4-T   C1-E

   one day you probably will—and maybe you'll even see a cat man."
                                                          A4-Z

60

Punctuation Puzzles & Mazes • Scholastic Professional Books

Name_____ **Date** _____

Maze

Directions: Trace a path from start to finish through nine areas that contain correctly punctuated and capitalized quotations. Avoid sentences that contain mistakes!

★ **Bonus:** In the entire maze, how many quotations are there that contain only correct capitalization and punctuation? ____

"Can we swim in the pond?" Asked Pat.

Jane said, "It's time to go."

"Yummy!" exclaimed Pia.

Finish

"Do swans migrate in winter," asked Anna?

Brenda cried, "The swan just bit my finger!"

"It's finally time to eat," Sighed Pia happily.

"Where," asked Freddie, "Does the swan sleep?"

Hint: Be careful: There are false paths that lead to dead ends.

"I wonder," said Fernando. "If the swan has a nearby nest."

"Swans are such regal birds!" exclaimed Mia.

"Is it true that swans mate for life?" asked Annelise.

Lucia exclaimed, "It's a beautiful bird on a beautiful day!"

"I think," said Sula, "that ducks are nice too."

Brenda asked, "Are all swans mute?"

"Will we be allowed to feed the swan?" Asked Alexander hopefullly.

"Sometimes," said Ted, "swans can drive away ducks and geese."

Start

"There are swans in fairy tales," said Nan.

"When's lunch?" asked Pia.

"Duck," yelled Thomas!

Min cried, "Wow!"

"I want to see it fly," Said Tanya.

"¡pəɹɐʌs ʎ

Ari asked, "What's its name?"

Pia said, "I'm hungry."

"Hey," shouted Pia, "I'm really starved."

"Look!" cried Rosalinda.

"Is she okay?"asked Di.

"I think," said Katya, "that the swan is tired."

Doris asked, "are swans smart birds?"

"I wish I could float just like that", sighed Eric.

"Why," whined Pia, "Doesn't anyone want to eat?"

Molly said, "Our mute swans originally came from Europe and Asia".

Unit 13: Review

The two puzzles in this unit review all the material covered in this book.

Teaching Tips

★ The dragon maze covers material from Units 1, 2, 3, 4, 5, 7, and 8 (correcting sentence fragments, correcting run-on sentences, the capitalization of proper nouns and adjectives, and using commas to set off adjective and adverb clauses).

★ The dinosaur maze covers material from Units 6, 9, 10, 11, and 12 (using commas to set off items in a series; direct addresses, parenthetical expressions, and unemphatic exclamations; and the punctuation and capitalization of quotations).

Answers

Page 63, Dragon Maze
The path to the end goes through: 1. If a dragon appeared, I'd run! **2.** The one that I see looks angry. **3.** Eastern and Western artists painted dragons. **4.** Dragons can fly, but they can also swim. **5.** This dragon, who seems very upset, is probably just about to breathe fire. **6.** There are dragons with lions' heads, and some have the heads of eagles. **7.** I like stories about knights; however, I often root for the dragon. **8.** In caves watch out for dragon lairs! **9.** Are there books about dragons if I want to know more? **10.** In May I read a dragon book. **11.** As you know, many fairy tales have dragons. **12.** One was big; the other was tiny. **13.** This, as you know, is a large dragon. **14.** Beowulf, who is the hero of an Old English saga, kills a dragon. **15.** Things that are unreal often seem very real to us. **16.** I wish my science teacher were here! **17.** Those who kiss dragons get burned. **18.** I met the dragon, and I lived to tell the tale!

Page 64, Dinosaur Maze
The path to the end goes through: 1. Farah said, "Many dinosaurs were, I'm sure, not really dangerous." **2.** "What nails!" cried Eve. **3.** "I may have nightmares," said Ron. **4.** "No, Sara, he's not friendly," said Dee. **5.** "Why," asked Marco, "did they all die out?" **6.** Some were huge, some were small, and some were tiny. **7.** Teeth, bones, and eggs have been found. **8.** "Kit, let's not get too close," said May. **9.** "Help me!" I cried. **10.** I said, "No, don't bite me!" **11.** "This," he said, "may be the end."

READY-TO-GO REPRODUCIBLES

Name_____ Date_____

Dragon Maze

Directions: Trace a path through 18 areas that contain complete sentences with correct punctuation and capitalization. Avoid any areas containing mistakes!

The one that I see looks angry.

Eastern and Western artists painted dragons.

This dragon, who seems very upset, is probably just about to breathe fire.

START

If a dragon appeared, I'd run!

Terrible fiery dragons!

Dragons can fly, but they can also swim.

There are dragons with lions' heads, and some have the heads of eagles.

Stand very still!

Some dragons like caves, others live on mountains.

Although most dragons are evil some in China are good.

Dragons like Lizards have scales.

I like stories about knights; however, I often root for the dragon.

Do dragons hibernate in the Winter?

Things that are unreal often seem very real to us.

Are there books about dragons if I want to know more?

In caves watch out for dragon lairs!

A griffin not a dragon.

St. George who was a knight killed a dragon.

When people are afraid they may create dragons.

I spotted one on Monday!

They like treasure, thus they horde gold.

In May I read a dragon book.

It's a french dragon.

One was big; the other was tiny.

This, as you know, is a large dragon.

A sweet tale of a dragon in love.

I wish my science teacher were here!

As you know, many fairy tales have dragons.

Beowulf, who is the hero of an Old English saga, kills a dragon.

Those who kiss dragons get burned.

I met the dragon, and I lived to tell the tale!

END

Name_____ Date_____

Dinosaur Maze

Directions: Trace a path through 11 areas that contain sentences with correct punctuation and capitalization. Avoid any areas containing mistakes!

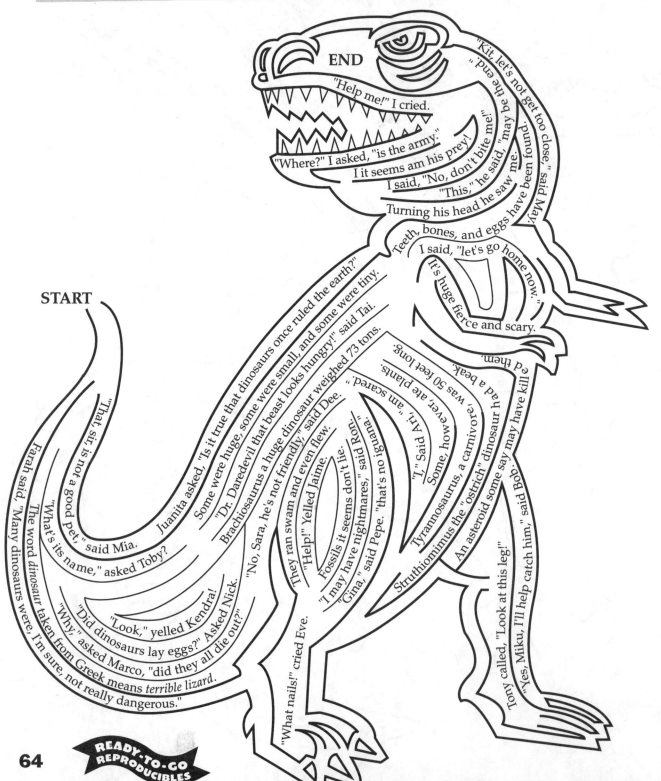

END

"Help me!" I cried.

"Where?" I asked, "is the army."

I it seems am his prey!

I said, "No, don't bite me!"

"This," he said, "may be the end."

"Kit, let's not get too close," said May.

Turning his head he saw me.

Teeth, bones, and eggs have been found.

I said, "let's go home now."

It's huge fierce and scary.

START

"That sir, is not a good pet," said Mia.

Farah said, "Many dinosaurs were, I'm sure, not really dangerous."

The word *dinosaur* taken from Greek means *terrible lizard.*

"Why," asked Marco, "did they all die out?"

"Did dinosaurs lay eggs?" Asked Marco.

"What's its name," asked Toby?

"Look," yelled Kendra!

Juanita asked, "Is it true that dinosaurs once ruled the earth?"

Some were huge, some were small, and some were tiny.

"Dr. Daredevil that beast looks hungry!" said Tai.

Brachiosaurus a huge dinosaur weighed 73 tons.

"No, Sara, he's not friendly," said Dee.

They ran swam and even flew.

"Help!" Yelled Jaime.

"What nails!" cried Eve.

Fossils it seems don't lie.

"I may have nightmares," said Ron.

"Gina," said Pepe, "that's no iguana."

"I, am scared." "I, Said Ari."

however, was 50 feet long.

Some, ate plants.

Tyrannosaurus, a carnivore, had a beak.

Struthiomimus the "ostrich" dinosaur ed them.

An asteroid some say may have kill

Tony called, "Look at this leg!"

"Yes, Miku, I'll help catch him," said Bob.

READY-TO-GO REPRODUCIBLES

Punctuation Puzzles & Mazes • Scholastic Professional Books